Comanches and Other Indians of Texas

Comanches
& Other Indians
of Texas

MARIAN T. PLACE

c. 1

Harcourt, Brace & World, Inc.
New York

Curriculum-Related Books are relevant to current interests of young people and to topics in the school curriculum.

PICTURE CREDITS

Maps by Raymond Houlihan: pp. 17, 34, 51, 73; Culver Pictures Inc.: pp. 24, 63, 93, 98, 100; Division of Manuscripts, University of Oklahoma Library: p. 119; New York Public Library: pp. 45, 86; Smithsonian Institution National Anthropological Archives: pp. 55, 121, 130; Texas Memorial Museum: p. 10a; United States Army Field Artillery Center and Fort Sill Museum, Fort Sill, Oklahoma: p. 123; University of Texas Institute of Texas Cultures, San Antonio: p. 10b.

First edition

Library of Congress Catalog Number: 79-103829

Printed in the United States of America

To Betty Allen

Contents

PART ONE

The Early Tribes

I

Early Man in Texas

ONE HOT DAY in June 1953 an amateur archeologist named Keith Glasscock trudged across the arid plain near Midland, in western Texas. The land was almost flat, except where the wind had built up sand dunes or scoured out large saucerlike depressions. Occasionally he stopped to explore one of these blowouts, hoping to find ancient stone points dropped there thousands of years ago by early big-game hunters. Like a prospector panning for gold, he tested one location after another, and recovered a number of flints and bits of fossilized bone. These told him that long ago, before sand dunes had choked the lake and marshes that once were there, early man had hunted now-extinct species of wolves, camels, and the three-toed horse in the area.

Finding the points was exciting, but similar ones had been found elsewhere in the state. Thus the goal of this man's patient searching—in spite of the discomforts of heat, thirst, sun glare, and blowing sand—was to find something so special that archeologists all over the country would take note. Actually, his chances of making a significant discovery were slim. Thousands of amateurs all over the continent—men, women, and schoolchildren—liked to dig for fossils and Indian artifacts.

Mr. Glasscock was to be one of the fortunate ones. Not long after he pocketed a Folsom point from the bottom of one blowout, he moved on to explore another. Here he stumbled on fragments of a human skeleton. He recognized them as being parts of a skull, rib, and hand. The wind had cut away the grayish sand in which they were imbedded. Dropping down on hands and knees, he picked them up, but only because they were in danger of being blown away. Other fragments, partially exposed, he left in place.

Because the particles were heavily fossilized, he realized at once that he had made an important discovery. Fossilized animal remains were fairly common throughout Texas, but those of early man were not. Then, unselfishly, Mr. Glasscock reported his find to an outstanding archeologist named Fred Wendorf. He and fellow scientists joined the discoverer at the site, which was located on a ranch owned by Clarence Scharbauer. There they conducted an exhaustive examination of this blowout and others. After weeks of cautious digging and months of very complicated, painstaking research in laboratories, they learned that the fragments were those of a woman, whom they quickly referred to as "Midland Minnie." She was about thirty years old when she died, some twelve thousand years ago. This was during the late Pleistocene Age when much of North America was covered by vast sheets of ice. The Midland fragments were extraordinary because they proved to be the oldest verified human fossil remains found in all the Americas. Archeologists expressed such interest in them that Mr. Wendorf and his associates wrote a small book about their work at the Scharbauer site and in their laboratories. It was published by the University of Texas Press under the title *The Midland Discovery*, and proved fascinating reading for either amateurs or scholars. However, the authors well knew that Midland Minnie's claim to fame might be superseded by other findings, because new "digs" from Alaska to the tip of South America are always being studied. They were right. In 1968 remains of human inhabitants that date back to 11,000 to 13,000 years ago were uncovered at the Marmes site in the Middle Snake River area of Washington.

Although thousands of years have passed since Midland Minnie's voice was stilled, her remains tell us some of the story of man's earliest appearance on the Texas plains. But we must go back farther in time to discover how this young woman and her family, remote antecedents of some of the later Indians of Texas, reached the Midland area, and how *her* forefathers came to the New World.

Geologists tell us that about thirty thousand years ago a land bridge connected the Old World with the New. This occurred as a sheet of ice ten thousand feet high inched down from the polar region. It was nourished by immense quantities of water drawn from the Arctic Ocean and Bering Sea, the shallow body of water separating Siberia from Alaska. After the wet, gravelly bed was exposed to sunlight, seeds borne there on the wind took root. The new land became carpeted with lush prairie grass. Meantime, many huge animals—including hairy elephants with curved tusks, giant bears, and deer—retreated from the ice encroaching on their Siberian pastureland. In their search for food, they grazed across the land bridge onto the central plateau of Alaska.

Stalking these great beasts were our earliest big-game hunters. Archeologists cannot tell us exactly when the first small family groups set foot in the New World. Some claim it was thirty thousand years ago; others insist it was much earlier. It was a fitful migration, extending over thousands of years by peoples of diverse racial stocks, some Mongoloid, some not.

Thanks to scientists who have located some ancient campsites, we now know in a general way that one route that early men and their descendants traveled went up the Yukon River valley, over to the Mackenzie River in western Canada, and down an ice-free corridor along the Rocky Mountains onto the Great Plains of the present American West. At least ten thousand years passed, and untold generations lived and died before these early peoples traveled the four thousand miles from the Bering Sea to West Texas. Other groups settled in what is now New Mexico and Arizona. Some pushed on through Central and South America until they stopped short of land's end, in a cave in Chile.

To simplify matters, let us call these first Americans "early big-game hunters." Some archeologists refer to them as Old Hunters, or Ancient Hunting Peoples, or Paleo-Americans, or Paleo-Indians. Since "paleo" is derived from a Greek word meaning "ancient," by Paleo-Indians they mean simply one of the primitive, prehistoric peoples of the New World. And although the experts might hem and haw and think it frivolous, it's fun to think of Midland Minnie as "the first Texan."

Before the Midland discovery, one of the earliest campsites frequented by man in America was found farther east near Lewisville, in Denton County, Texas. Ancient hearths examined by members of the Dallas Archeological Society yielded bits of charcoal, the charred remains of extinct animals, and, most exciting, a crude flint spear point later identified as a "Clovis fluted point." Similar ones have been found all the way from Alaska to Texas, and especially near Clovis, New Mexico. They are leaf-shaped with a broad shallow channel, or flute, on one or both sides, running from the base half way to the tip. They range from $1\frac{1}{2}$ to 5 inches long, and from one-third to one-half that in width, and are usually found in association with the remains of extinct elephants. From the Lewisville discoveries and others, experts were able to deduce that a now-extinct species of elephant roamed the Staked Plains (*Llano Estacado*) of Texas, and that the early big-game hunters killed them near their water holes about twelve thousand years ago.

This date was not guessed at, but estimated after the bone and charcoal fragments were examined in a lengthy, very complex method known as radiocarbon dating. Briefly, it works this way. All living things absorb minute amounts of a form of carbon called carbon 14 from the atmosphere. At death, the living matter stops adding to its store, and the amount it contains starts to disintegrate at a uniform rate. Half of the C^{14} content disintegrates in 5,760 years, and half of the remainder in another similar period, and so on. Thus, scientists can measure the amount of C^{14} left in a fragment of ancient bone, for example, compare it to the amount of C^{14} in a present-day bone, and then calculate approximately how many years have passed since that bit of once-living tissue died. The figure arrived at is never exact, and is written thus: 12,000 ± 500, meaning in this case twelve thousand plus-or-minus five hundred years.

A discovery in the valley of Yellow House Draw, near Lubbock, yielded another kind of point, which was in use from about seven to nine thousand years ago. Members of the Texas Memorial Museum removed fifteen feet of overburden to uncover charred bison bones, which were radiocarbon dated at 9,883 ± 350 years. Amid them was a smaller, more beautifully made point. It, too, is more or less leaf-shaped, but broadest toward the tip, with a broad groove on one or both faces. The first of these points was found near Folsom, New Mexico, in 1925, and named for that location. Folsom fluted points range from less than one inch to about three inches in length. Another Folsom site, in Lipscomb County, Texas, yielded eighteen points, and countless others have turned up elsewhere.

In the summer of 1944 two geologists found a fossil bone in a gravel pit at Plainview. Later, members of the Texas Memorial Museum excavated the remains of nearly one hundred now-extinct species of bison from an area five hundred feet square. They also found several flint tools and a point that could not be classified as either Clovis or Folsom. After much study it was named the Plainview point. Although no human bones were found near it, the workmanship of the flint tools indicates that Plainview man was a skilled implement-maker and hunter.

One of the loneliest, wildest sections of Texas stretches along the Rio Grande River west of San Antonio. Distant mountains form dim blue barriers across the horizon, and vast acres dotted with greasewood end only at the river's edge. From two to eight thousand years ago shallow caves in the canyon walls sheltered a few primitive families. In 1933 an expedition from the Witte Memorial Museum of San Antonio excavated layer upon layer of debris left by these West Texas cave dwellers. They were a sedentary people, who used hooks made of cactus thorns or yucca-fiber nets to obtain fish. They discharged spears from throwing-sticks to down running animals such as rabbits, and gathered seeds and berries on the plain above the cliffs. The women were very skilled at weaving baskets and a coarse cloth of yucca fibers to fashion skirts and cloaks. Burial sites found in small caves yielded caches of seeds, clay pots, the body of an infant beneath a broken cradle, a net of twisted sotol fiber, stone knives, and beads made from the vertebrae of rattlesnakes. Faintly seen on the walls were crude drawings of animals and the human hand. Experts still are not sure why the cave dwellers died out. Possibly they died during an epidemic, or were killed by plains raiders from the north. Their remains may be seen at the museum of the West Texas Historical Society at Alpine.

An entire book could be written about the many evidences of the presence of the early big-game hunters in Texas. But since they fit closely those already described, mention will be made of only one more discovery, not far from Dallas. In 1929 a crew digging gravel five miles west of Malakoff found a rounded boulder that bore cuts representing the face of a man. It was of sandstone, 16 inches long and about 14 inches wide, and weighed slightly over 98 pounds. On it were plainly carved the eyes, nose, mouth, and chin of some ancient man. The stone created much excitement among archeologists because none like it had been found elsewhere in the United States.

In 1935 a second, smaller stone was found nearby, and a third in the original pit. It is impossible to gaze upon these old, old stones without feeling that here are the faces of ancient men staring at us from across a time still shrouded in mystery. No flint points or animal remains were uncovered in the pits to provide a clue to the people who carved the stones. But they do tell us this—if man had time to carve something other than a tool or weapon, he must have developed skills that allowed him some small measure of relief from the ever-pressing need to hunt for food.

In time, early man and the beasts he hunted died out. No one knows why this happened. Apparently as the herds of bison increased, the elephant and camel and early horse became extinct. Slowly new people drifted down into present-day Texas. They were the forefathers of the Indians encoun-

On this stone head, found near Malakoff, Texas, are carved the clearly distinguishable features of a man. Two similar stones were also found.

Fossilized bone fragments of Midland Minnie's skull were found to be those of a young woman who died about twelve thousand years ago.

tered by Spanish explorers. Archeologists label theirs the "Archaic culture," meaning a way of life belonging to a former or older period. Archaic men gained in strength and numbers, fashioned more complicated tools and pottery, developed the bow and arrow, planted corn and beans, and improved their dwellings. After thousands of years they came together in larger groups, and tribal organizations resulted.

Today we call their descendants the Indians of Texas.

II

The Karankawas

ONE DAY after another in the autumn of 1519 was much the same for the lean, brown-skinned natives who lived at the mouth of the Rio Grande River. The sun was bright but veiled in a pearly haze, the air balmy, the sandy shoreline gently washed by low white breakers rolling in from the Gulf of Mexico. Time had no sharp edges here. The people did not recall when their forefathers first came to the big brown river and green Gulf. Both offered food aplenty in the form of fish, crabs, and oysters. The nests of shorebirds yielded fresh eggs, and the sand dunes edible plants. So the people had settled there, raised shelters of mud and reeds, and attuned their lives to the rhythm and harvests of the seasons.

As years rolled into decades and centuries, family groups increased. Newcomers wandered into their midst from the north, west, and south. Some wanted to fight; others were sociable. By the dawn of the sixteenth century there were forty villages extending up the riverbank a distance of twenty miles. Now and then itinerant peddlers arrived on foot, and swapped shells with cutting edges for dart points, bright feathers, bits of turquoise, baskets, bowls, even a gold amulet. The peddlers tarried long enough to pass along news gathered during their visits with villagers living as much as a thousand miles or more upstream. They told of people who dwelt in caves or in handsome multi-storied pueblos surrounded by plantings of corn, beans, squash, and melons. Thus the natives at the mouth of the Rio Grande knew something of their distant neighbors.

One of the lessons the natives had learned from tragic experience was that danger could erupt from any direction landward, in the form of war parties who raided for slaves. Only from the east was there no danger. During the storm season the people had to leave the white beach and seek shelter among the dunes and palm groves, but otherwise the world to their east was friendly, home of the sun and fish-filled Gulf waters.

But one day in that autumn of 1519, either fishermen hauling in nets or perhaps children romping with their dogs on the beach spied four dark objects looming on the eastern horizon. At first they were thought to be clouds. Then, as they came nearer, the astonished natives guessed that they were houses floating on the water. After tacking back and forth in the wind, as birds do, the four strange craft slipped over a sand bar and entered the river proper. Smaller boats were lowered, and men clambered down into them for the short haul to the beach. What strange creatures they were! Light-skinned, their faces adorned with hair that was black, gold, or even red, wearing shining pieces of armor over shirts or suits of brocade and velvet, their legs encased in leather coverings, their hands brandishing metal weapons. One man, obviously the leader, stepped into the shallow water, slashed through a wave with a gleaming sword, then thrust it into the sand and made a short speech in a strange tongue.

This was Captain Alonso Alvarez de Piñeda, commander of

four ships and two hundred and seventy Spanish gentlemen and soldiers. He had been dispatched by the Spanish governor of Jamaica to sail along the shores of "Florida," which then included all the land fronting the Gulf of Mexico. The captain hoped to locate a water passage to the Orient. By running his sword through the water and sand, he took possession of both on behalf of the king of Spain.

During the next forty days he visited and traded with the friendly brown-skinned natives, and explored upstream past forty more "towns." He named the broad placid muddy stream the *Río de las Palmas*, after the tall palm trees along its banks. Then, after his ships had been repaired, and fish and fresh water taken aboard, the captain set sail for the return voyage to Jamaica. He had not found the short cut to the Orient. He did not leave men on shore to establish a colony. He was not more than casually interested in the natives. Only from his ship's log and a meager journal do we have a record of this first encounter between white men and the Indians of a future Texas.

The coming of Alvarez de Piñeda had little impact on the natives. (They were part of a widely-scattered tribe, the Coahuiltecans, who will be described in the following chapter.) An important and more widely known contact between white men and Indians occurred nine years later at a different place, and involved people of another tribe, the Karankawas.

In November 1528, Indians camped on a sand reef near present-day Galveston Island spied strangers on their shore. The newcomers were a sorry-looking group, their white bodies weathered by sun and salt air and gaunt from months of near starvation. A wild rolling sea had cast their boats ashore. Frightened, weak, shivering in the cold wind, they had staggered out of the pounding surf, gathered driftwood, and huddled about a fire.

Their plight was a far cry from what they had anticipated when they joined the expedition of Pánfilo de Narváez. The arrogant, red-headed Spanish adventurer had set forth to conquer the country between the Florida peninsula and eastern Mexico, and wrest vast quantities of gold and precious gems from the natives. However, a series of misfortunes had cost many lives and deprived the survivors of all their belongings. None had gained the wealth and slaves hoped for, and the tattered desperate men warming themselves by the fire were destitute now and without a leader, for the boat transporting Narváez had disappeared in the storm.

More bad luck awaited the survivors. In looking around, they found themselves surrounded by a hundred warriors. The natives were six feet tall, well-formed brown-skinned men, impressively armed with cedar bows. Since the Spaniards obviously were helpless and unarmed, and made no hostile gestures, the Indians were friendly. They helped the castaways travel the short distance to their huts. Here they shared their scant supply of roots and fish, and entertained their guests by dancing and singing until dawn.

We know this because, fortunately for history's sake, one of the Spaniards was a remarkable man named Álvar Núñez Cabeza de Vaca. After eight difficult years of exile among the Indians of Texas, he returned to civilization and wrote at length of his experiences. Thus we have a fascinating picture of primitive peoples and the far-flung wilderness from which they eked out a miserable existence.

Cabeza de Vaca described his companions' first impression of the natives by writing, "if they were not large, our fears made giants of them." He does not say how the sun-blistered Europeans, their lips swollen and bleeding, their hair and beards matted, their eyes inflamed by wind and salt spray, must have appeared to their savage hosts. Because the Spaniards' boats were wrecked, they were forced to remain on the island. They named it "*la isla de mal hado*" or Bad Luck Island. Modern-day historians would argue whether this was Galveston Island or a smaller one called San Luis Island. Of the eighty who were flung ashore, by the following spring only fifteen remained. Four had left to try and reach a Mexican settlement, hoping to return with a rescue ship, but they were never seen again. Sixty-one died of hardship or disease. Before they were buried in the sand, the flesh from their thin flanks was cut away, dried, and eaten by their starving countrymen.

As time passed, the wretched survivors were parceled out as slaves among the neighboring bands, and saw nothing of each other for six years. Cabeza de Vaca was one of these. For many months he remained with the island people, communicating as best he could in sign language until he could converse haltingly in their guttural speech. He called them Capoques, or Cahoques. They were related to the Karankawa tribe, and roamed the offshore islands and flat grassy shoreland, or coastal prairie, from the west shore of Galveston Bay to the mouth of the Brazos River. The Karankawas proper circulated about Matagorda Bay, while other small bands ranged as far south as the mouth of the Nueces River. Modern scholars tell us the word "Karankawa" probably meant "dog-lovers," and might have been given them because their villages were overrun with packs of dogs. Although some were pets, no doubt during starving times many a dog was roasted and eaten.

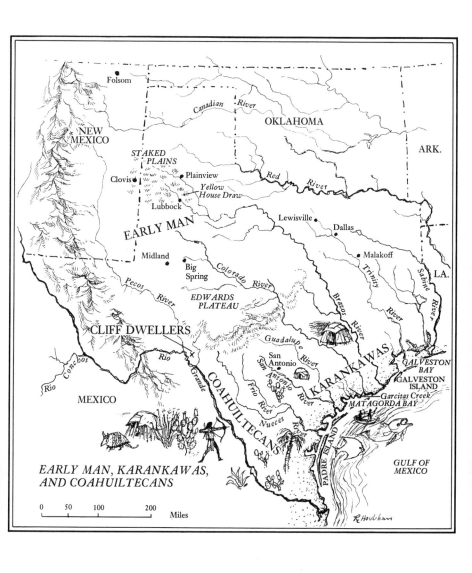

EARLY MAN, KARANKAWAS,
AND COAHUILTECANS

0   50   100   200
|____|____|_____| Miles

The Spaniards' impression that the Karankawa warriors were giants was not too far-fetched. Europeans who saw them a century or more later also described the men as being tall and physically handsome, though the women were fat and stooped from a lifetime of drudgery. Men and boys went naked, but the women and girls wore short skirts made from deerskin and streamers of Spanish moss. To differentiate the members of the various bands, both sexes tattooed their bodies, or painted on colored stripes or figures resembling birds and flowers. They also punctured the outer edges of the nostrils, ear lobes, and lower lips in order to dangle beads, shells, or bits of reed from them. The men wore their dark hair in a single long braid bound with rawhide and the tail of a rattlesnake.

Cabeza de Vaca found them hospitable and merry in the face of continuing poverty and hardship. Although later accounts brand them as fierce-looking cannibals, he does not. In fact, he states that the Capoques were disgusted when his starving comrades ate the flesh of those who had died. The early Anglo-American and German white settlers were wary of them not only because of their reputation for cannibalism, but because they were an unattractive people. Noah Smithwick, who arrived in 1827, wrote, "Their ugly faces were rendered hideous by the alligator grease and dirt with which they were besmeared from head to foot as a defense against mosquitoes." Apparently the Texas pioneers found the name Karankawa difficult to pronounce, because they nicknamed them "Kronks."

An explanation of the Karankawas' being labeled cannibals is provided by a noted Texas anthropoligist, W. W. Newcomb, Jr. In his book *The Indians of Texas from Prehistoric to Modern Times*, Mr. Newcomb states ". . . the cannibalism they practiced was distinct from the custom of eating human flesh simply as food. Many American Indians and most Texas natives ate bits and pieces of their dead or dying enemies. This custom was due not to hunger but was motivated by magic or revenge."

Although modern readers like to think of Indians as being "free as a bird" to roam whenever and wherever they pleased, this is not so. True, most nomadic tribes did move about, but they were captives of their requirements for food and the skins needed for clothing and shelters. Even when they came to an ideal campsite, they could stay only as long as the local food supply lasted. Their travels also were limited by the amount of hunting territory they could hold against the inroads of enemy tribes.

The Karankawas lived a miserable existence fraught with constant pressure to obtain food and, at times, drinking water. When Cabeza de Vaca arrived on the scene, they were catching fish. Since they lacked hooks and their dugouts were too unstable to take out into deep water, they used weirs woven of reeds to trap the fish. Or the men stood hip deep in the water, arrow strung to the bow, absolutely motionless, until a flounder, porpoise, or redfish swam within range. Then they shot with remarkable accuracy, lifted the fish to remove the arrow, and tossed it on shore. The women cleaned the fish with sharp cutting tools made of oyster shells. After throwing the entrails to the dogs, they wrapped the fish in kelp and baked them on a bed of slow-burning driftwood.

They lived in huts called ba-aks, which were little more than windbreaks. The average dwelling was about twelve feet in diameter, made of a framework of poles covered with mats and skins, and housing about eight individuals. In the spring the women dismantled the shelters and all ferried to the mainland in the dugouts, which were propelled by poles. The huts were raised again, and then the women and children set to work gathering oysters, clams, mussels, turtles, and marine plants. Shellfish were cooked over hot coals until the shells opened and the succulent meat could be removed with pointed sticks. Meanwhile, the men hunted alligators for their tough white meat and hides. A strong-smelling grease rendered from the fat was used liberally as a mosquito repellent.

After the wild geranium bloomed, the foragers moved inland a short distance to feast on black dewberries, herbs, wild onions, and the tuna, or fruit of the wild prickly pear. In addition they ate very large spiders, worms, snakes, lizards, and rats. When the broiling summer heat moderated, the men paddled up the streams a short distance and stalked deer, antelope, javelina, or wild boar, and an occasional bison, popularly misnamed buffalo.

Following a successful hunt, the men expressed their thanks not in prayers but in drinking bouts. For such occasions the women toasted the leaves of the yaupon, an evergreen shrub, in an earthen pot, and then added boiling water. The scalding drink was poured into halves of gourds, whipped to a froth, and then drunk and vomited at the rate of five gallons per day per adult!

The Karankawas were a sociable people who intermarried freely among a half-dozen bands. They shared a common language but otherwise were independent, with no cohesive tribal organization or chief over all. Each band was presided over by a chief chosen for his bravery and fortitude. The honor need not be hereditary. Occasionally the bands came together for a celebration when summoned by messengers or smoke signals. Apparently marriages were arranged following a proffering of gifts by the suitor to his sweetheart's parents. The young couple joined the husband's family and band. The wife was not restricted in her social relations with her in-laws, but her husband dared not visit or even look eye-to-eye with his wife's parents. They, in turn, could not enter their daughter's hut or interfere with the way the couple were raising their children.

Children were treated with affection. They were given two names, one used in public and another kept secret because it was supposed to possess magical power. The younger children helped in gathering food. As they grew older, the boys were taught to hunt and fish, and the girls to prepare food and clothing, make pottery, and weave baskets. The boys had small bows and arrows, first for play and later for training. The girls used crudely carved sticks of wood for dolls. Both adults and children loved to sing and dance, but the ceremonial dances were enjoyed only by the men.

Scholars tell us the Karankawas worshiped the sun through two deities named Pichini and Mel, and honored them with ceremonies and dances. When children or warriors died, the families spent a year in mourning. The dead were buried in shallow graves along with their favorite trinkets or tools. An elderly person's passing was not an occasion for sorrow, because the people felt they were better off after being released from the hardships of daily living.

Karankawa warriors liked to fight against neighboring tribes. Their principal weapons were bows and arrows, though on occasion they used heavy clubs. When raiding for scalps or slaves, they were extremely savage. They exhibited great skill in defending themselves and their people from attacks. Usually a village was located on the edge of a stand of timber or a dense thicket. All helped dig trenches around the outer perimeter and covered the openings with branches. The warriors alternately slept and maintained guard duty in them. A narrow, well-camouflaged path led into the woods where the women and children lived. Often deceptive fires were lighted to attract the enemy, and when a raiding party appeared, it was ambushed and slaughtered.

As mentioned earlier, the Karankawas were friendly to the survivors of the Narváez expedition. Afterwards they turned hostile to whites who trespassed on their territory. In 1685 a French expedition led by Robert Cavelier, Sieur de La Salle, reached Matagorda Bay and established a tiny fort along Garcitas Creek. When the natives stole some blankets washed ashore from the wreckage of one of the ships, the Frenchmen killed them. Further contacts with Spanish settlers and missionaries occurred during the late eighteenth and early nineteenth centuries. However, the relationship was never friendly, largely owing to the harsh treatment the Spaniards inflicted on the Indians.

Never a large tribe, the independent Karankawa bands slowly lost numbers through the diseases introduced by Europeans, and as a result of the seizure of their land by early white settlers. After attacking a small settlement on the Guadalupe River in 1844, some of the Karankawas fled to the sandy wastes of Padre Island. Others drifted into Mexico, and Texas saw no more of this very early native people.

III

The Coahuiltecans

SEVEN YEARS after being cast ashore on Bad Luck Island, Cabeza de Vaca got in touch with the four remaining survivors of the Narváez expedition. Three were Spaniards, and the fourth a Negro slave. All determined to end their lonely exile among capricious savages. After much cautious planning they slipped away and headed for Mexico, where they hoped to find fellow countrymen. Several days later one of the Spaniards dropped out. The others pressed on, and encountered a weak, half-starved band of Coahuiltecan Indians. They were friendly but had no food to offer other than baked leaves of the prickly pear. Since it was September and the land was parched under the pitiless sun, there was no drinking water. Thirst and hunger drove the Spaniards to eat the unripened fruit of the pear. The milky juice burned their swollen, cracked lips and intensified their thirst, while the pulp brought on violent stomach cramps. Next they bargained for two skinny dogs and consumed them flesh and blood. Somewhat revived, they trudged on only to meet other equally deprived bands.

Like the neighboring Karankawas, the Coahuiltecans were descendants of Archaic hunters. There were over two hun-

After their escape from the Karankawas, Cabeza de Vaca and his companions met many groups of Indians, including Coahuiltecans and Jumanos, on their wanderings through Texas.

dred bands and sub-groups included in this western Gulf culture area. The better-known ones were the Payayas, who lived near present-day San Antonio, the Aranams, Orejons, Pachals, Yguazes, Arbadaos, and the Borrados, whom Alvarez de Piñeda had met in 1519. They ranged through a vast sunscorched region of brush and cactus extending from present-day San Antonio and the Guadalupe River, along the Frio and Nueces, to the Rio Grande, adjoining the Mexican states Nueva León and Coahuila. Little of their prehistoric past is known. Once they adapted themselves to living in the brush country of South Texas, their culture remained extremely primitive, because their energies and talents were concentrated on surviving. Having no agriculture, they were constantly on the move to obtain food from this prickly, unproductive region.

Cabeza de Vaca mentioned that the Yguazes were fine archers, and some could pursue a deer at a running trot for hours without tiring. They were not as tall as the Karankawas, but did wear breechclouts and fiber sandals. During the cold months they donned cloaks made of coyote hides. Each band and sub-group had a singular tattoo, to distinguish its members from others. Their portable huts and use of trenches to defend their villages were similar to the Karankawas'. Although the latter could not have been too clean, the Coahuiltecan villages were filthy by comparison.

Because sustaining life was a struggle, the bands lived in closely knit groups. All shared in the work. A successful hunter kept only the hide of his kill, the remains being turned over to the group. Each band had its chief and shaman, or medicine man. Otherwise all families had equal social status, and none enjoyed more privileges or food than the others.

Often messengers carried challenges to enemy Karankawan

camps with a summons to fight. Such an emissary would deck himself in his war regalia and present himself to the chief of the adversary camp, shoot an arrow into a tree, and stomp about in a war dance. If the chief wanted to fight, he had one of his men behave similarly. The messenger ran home but returned soon with his comrades to do battle. If successful, the warriors impaled the scalps they had taken atop poles, set the poles in the ground, and whooped and danced about them. Any captives taken were killed, roasted, and eaten.

Cabeza de Vaca noted that Coahuiltecan marriages and child-rearing customs were about the same as the Karankawas, but added "they have not so great love for their children as those we have before spoken of." Both boys and girls were subjected to painful tattooing. This was done by making shallow incisions with a sharpened shell or flint, and rubbing charcoal and resin into the cuts. The children were forbidden to cry out during this painful ordeal.

Necessity made plant-food experts of the Coahuiltecans, because they had so few natural resources available. Within their band's territories they roamed constantly, gathering roots, nuts, seeds, and fruit, and hunting deer, javelina, and an occasional bison. Communal hunts were popular. For these, all able-bodied persons of several bands surrounded a herd of deer or a large number of rabbits, and drove them into a small circle where the hunters could slaughter them easily. Invariably the hunts were celebrated in gluttonous feasting. In contrast, fishing was carried on by small parties who trapped the fish, or used lighted torches at night to lure the fish within range of their bows and arrows. The fish were either roasted without cleaning and allowed to become thoroughly rotten and infested with insects before being eaten, or the flesh and bones were dried and pounded into a sort of flour. Other sources of food included spiders, lizards, snakes, ant eggs, and bulbs roasted or ground into flour.

The people living along the Nueces River and lower Rio Grande harvested vast quantities of the tender, sweet, and nutritious beans from the mesquite tree. Usually the beans were stripped from the pods and eaten or pounded into flour, but the Arbadaos had a quite different way of preparing them. The women dug a hole in the ground, threw in some beans, and pounded them with a club. Earth from the sides of the hole was mixed in, and often a different and special earth was dropped in by the handful. Then the coarse flour was placed in a pot, water added, and the broth thickened by the addition of more earth. The people scooped this up in their hands, and consumed it with great relish.

The Coahuiltecans were so impoverished that their bows were made of mesquite root, and the bowstrings from plant fibers or deer sinew. The arrows were of cane, with flint points. Knives and scrapers were flint. The women of some bands wove baskets and nets from plant fibers, dried gourds for storing flour, and used wooden sticks for grubbing out roots, bulbs, and insects.

The people believed in spirits. Religious ceremonies and festivals, called *mitotes,* were supervised by shamans, who indulged in tricks of magic and sleight-of-hand to impress the celebrants. The *mitotes* featured night-long singing and dancing. During the feasting peyote was either eaten or used in making an intoxicating drink. The base of peyote is the spineless mescal cactus, of which only the dried upper part is used. Supposedly it heightens one's perceptions and produces hallucinations, but is not habit-forming. Among a people who set great store by dreams and visions, its use was popular and widespread. (Although the old-time *mitotes* have died out, peyote is still used by some modern American Indians in the West in religious observances.)

When Cabeza de Vaca and his companions reached the Colorado River of Texas where it empties into Matagorda Bay, they turned inland along a well-worn Indian trail. Runners from the various villages they encountered carried word of their coming to those beyond, so singing delegations often advanced to welcome them. The exiles visited present-day Big Spring, then gradually worked across South Texas to the confluence of the Rio Grande and the Conchos. After a long trek across what is now New Mexico and Arizona, they turned south into Mexico and finally reached their countrymen.

The Coahuiltecans saw nothing of other Spaniards for about a hundred years. Gradually, as Spanish settlements were established south of the Rio Grande River, Catholic priests moved out to found missions as far north as San Antonio. The Coahuiltecans accepted Christianity and mission life, and became less warlike. But they steadily lost numbers to white men's diseases. In the mid-eighteenth century many were killed by raiding Apaches and Comanches. The handful of survivors drifted into northern Mexico, and by 1900 the Coahuiltecans had disappeared from the Texas scene.

IV

The Jumanos

CABEZA DE VACA and other Spaniards who journeyed through southwestern Texas during the sixteenth century encountered natives whom they named Jumanos. The meaning of the term is not known, and there is less information about them than all other Texas Indians. They are included here because they were the only pueblo dwellers within the present state.

Archeologists tell us there were two groups, and they were geographically distinct. One was made up of barbaric gardeners living in pueblos, the other of nomadic hunters on the southwestern Texas plains. Whether or not they spoke the same language and evolved from the same early people can only be guessed. Generally speaking, they were seen from below El Paso to the confluence of the Conchos and the Rio Grande. The Spaniards called the junction of these rivers "La Junta de los Ríos." One of the principal freight routes from Mexico City into Texas, the Chihuahua Trail, followed down the Conchos and crossed the Rio Grande to present-day Presidio.

Centuries earlier people identified with the Pueblo culture had established themselves in the desert and canyon country of the American southwest. Possibly by 1000 A.D. a number of farming villages had come into being along the Rio Grande, extending more than a hundred miles below El Paso. By 1400 A.D. there were others on down to La Junta de los Rios. At what point the slowly migrating Pueblo people encountered local Archaic Indians is not known. But a new culture evolved from this contact. It adapted the habits and skills of both peoples to the region's harsh environment, and finally developed into what is now called the Jumano culture.

Cabeza de Vaca provided few details of them because, as he wrote, "We traveled through so many sorts of people, of such diverse languages, the memory fails to recall them." But he did say of those at La Junta, "We asked how it was they did not plant maize. They answered it was that they might not lose what they should put into the ground; that the rains had failed for two years in succession." He also referred to them as the "cow nation" because they were well supplied with the dried meat and hides of the buffalo. He did not witness a buffalo hunt since this activity was carried on by the nomadic Jumanos living north of the distant mountains.

In 1581 an expedition led by Father Rodríguez traveled northward through Mexico to convert the Indians living along the Rio Grande, and on into present New Mexico. The missionary party included two other priests, nine soldiers, nineteen Indian servants, six hundred head of cattle, and ninety horses. Hernán Gallegos, narrator for the expedition, wrote that they tarried at several *rancherías*, or villages, in the vicinity of La Junta and guessed the total population was about ten thousand. Modern scholars feel this figure is greatly exaggerated, that only one-third as many lived there. The people were handsome, painted their faces, and appeared to be happy and carefree.

Their adobe-brick houses were not the extraordinary multi-storied dwellings identified with the Pueblo Indians of the canyon country further west. They were separate one-story units set in the ground. The corner posts were made of cottonwood poles, the walls of adobe brick, and the flat roofs of ocotillo stalks thickly plastered. During the heat of the day the people stayed inside the cool shadowy interior, and emerged late in the day to eat and sleep on the roofs.

At La Junta, the Jumanos planted their crops on the floor of the narrow valleys enclosing both rivers. Since they practiced no form of irrigation, they depended on rainfall or water carried from the streams to their gardens. Close by were steep, gravelly terraces dotted with cacti and brush, and beyond these a wide border of desert land which gave way to mountains. Here the nomadic hunting Jumanos roamed, living off big game indigenous to the pine- and cedar-forested slopes. A few bands pushed farther north to hunt buffalo, and brought back hides and dried meat to trade with the valley dwellers. If the Jumanos followed Pueblo traditions, the men must have tended the crops. The women carried on their household tasks, which included making pottery and weaving baskets. They had few tools, and their weapons included bows and arrows, war clubs, and battle shields fashioned from tough buffalo hides.

Since the missionary priests did not settle at La Junta, the people there sent emissaries to the Franciscan mission at El Paso and urged that priests be sent to them. Eventually their request was granted. On June 12, 1684, on the banks of Alamito Creek, the formal establishment of a mission was completed. Some time after 1830 the name of La Junta de los Ríos was changed to Presidio del Norte (Fort of the North), and later shortened to Presidio.

One by one the pueblos lost population as continuing periods of drought lessened the harvests of crops. Some Jumanos drifted southward to work in Mexican mines and intermarried with Mexican Indians. Others adapted to the nomadic hunting life and reached out onto the southern plains and upper Red River region. According to Spanish sources, by the close of the sixteenth century the Jumanos dominated the country surrounding the upper Red and Canadian rivers. They made life so miserable for the Apaches, who were trying to establish themselves there, that the Apaches appealed to the leader of a Spanish military expedition to negotiate a peace for them with the Jumanos. If this was accomplished, it had little effect on either party. From about 1620 to 1660 the nomadic Jumanos were lords of the West Texas plains. Then slowly they began to lose out to the Apaches.

When La Salle encountered the Jumanos in 1686, he reported them as being strong, warlike, mounted, and journeying regularly into Mexico to trade for or steal horses and Spanish goods. These were traded to their allies, the Caddoan-speaking Tejas of East Texas. But during the early years of the eighteenth century they suffered such costly raids from the Apaches that they gradually merged with them, or with the Tejas, until their identity as Jumanos frittered away. They are remembered chiefly for the aspects of Pueblo culture that they brought to the varied and complex picture of Texas Indians.

V

The Atakapans

THE MARSHY SOUTHEAST COAST of Texas, ranging from the lower San Jacinto River and east shore of Galveston Bay to the Sabine River, was occupied by a people now called Atakapans. The word means "man-eaters." The earliest written record of them is contained in Cabeza de Vaca's journal. After he and his comrades landed on Bad Luck Island in 1528, he soon realized there were two villages there, which were seasonal homes to two separate peoples. The Capoques, already described, were Karankawas. The others, whom he called Hans but who are thought to have been Akokisas, were Atakapan Indians. Linguistically they were related to Indians who lived farther east in Louisiana, but culturally they were very much like the Karankawas. They got along well with the latter, but warred in a small way with their neighbors to the north, the Caddoes.

The Atakapans were said to be short and stout, dark-skinned and ugly. They kept their dark, dirty hair cropped, and tattooed themselves to such an extent that some of the cuts on the head and chin were almost deforming. Their teeth were stained from chewing some leaf. Europeans who visited them later mentioned their having very large ears and promi-

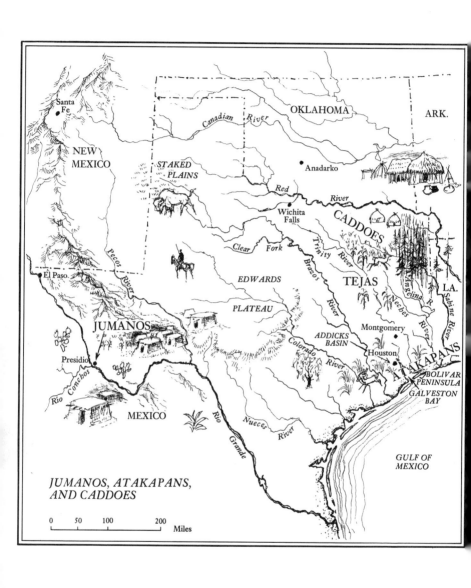

Santa Fe

NEW MEXICO

OKLAHOMA

ARK.

Canadian River

STAKED PLAINS

Anadarko

Red River

Wichita Falls

CADDOES

Clear Fork

Trinity River

Pecos River

El Paso

EDWARDS

Brazos River

TEJAS

Angelina R.

LA.

PLATEAU

JUMANOS

Neches River

Sabine River

Montgomery

ADDICKS BASIN

Colorado River

Houston

ATAKAPANS

Presidio

Rio Conchos

MEXICO

Rio Grande

Nueces River

BOLIVAR PENINSULA

GALVESTON BAY

GULF OF MEXICO

JUMANOS, ATAKAPANS, AND CADDOES

0   50   100   200
                              Miles

nent noses. The men usually wore only breechclouts but in winter draped themselves in buffalo skins with the tails left on and trailing behind. Their shirts were of deerskin and fastened with rawhide lacings.

Their dwellings were little more than brush shelters, and extremely verminous and dirty. When necessary, cooking could be done under cover in a shallow pit lined with broken oyster shells. The smoke escaped through a hole in the roof. Food and water were carried in skin containers, or in crude pots.

Almost nothing is known of Atakapan social organization. The various Texas bands (there were others in Louisiana) moved about seasonally in order to gather food. The Akokisas dwelt in four or five villages along the lower San Jacinto and Trinity rivers and the Gulf Coast. Upriver on the San Jacinto were the Patiris, and farther up the Trinity were the Bidais. All told, the people probably numbered no more than 3500 persons.

Perhaps because the Akokisas were such unattractive people, Cabeza de Vaca paid them little attention. However, in 1719 a French officer found himself stranded among them, and his observations were more detailed. This was twenty-four-year-old Simars de Bellisle, who had elected to serve as a gentleman officer aboard a French military and supply ship sent to support French expeditions penetrating eastern Texas.

Young Simars and four fellow officers were sent ashore in a small rowboat to refill the ship's water casks. Since this would take several days, they were supplied with guns and ammunition, and silver tableware. They were dressed in hats, coats, breeches, stockings, and boots. They landed near the mouth of the Trinity River, and had no trouble finding fresh water or in killing enough deer to feed themselves.

When the casks were filled, they waited on the beach for their ship, which had continued westward along the coast, to heave in sight. They waited and waited, in vain. The young men used up all their ship's biscuit, and ammunition, and slowly began to starve. One after another died until only Simars was left. He wrote later, "When I knew myself alone, I died a hundred deaths every quarter of an hour."

Not long after, he discovered a mess of fat yellow worms under a fallen tree. He built a fire with his flint starter, roasted them, and found they tasted quite good.

Some days later he spied Indians on an island not far off shore. Hoping they had food to spare, he rowed over. The Indians seized his possessions, stripped him naked, and subjected him to much abuse. Finally, a woman accepted him as a combination husband and slave. He was made to haul wood and water, and when he lagged, she beat him.

In the fall the Indians rowed to the mainland and slowly hunted their way northward along the Trinity River. Of this country he wrote, "This is the most beautiful country in the world. The earth is almost black. Grass grows there to a prodigal height and in abundance." Still farther north the Akokisas reached the village of the Bidais, to whom many were related by marriage. The Akokisas displayed their prize captive. By cajoling and trickery, Bellisle managed to write some sort of message, which Bidais hunters carried on a buffalo hunt in order to show it to other Indians as proof that they did possess a white captive. The message passed from hand to hand until, miraculously, it reached a French trader who was able to bring about his countryman's rescue.

Included in the account of his experiences among the Atakapan Indians is this short paragraph, which proves how well they deserved their reputation as cannibals. The Akokisas had made a successful raid on a Caddo hunters' camp. "When they returned, they threw this Indian on the prairie. One of them cut his head off and another one cut the arms off, while they skinned him at the same time. Several of them ate the yellow fat, which was still raw, and finally they devoured him completely."

The Bidais, whose name means "people of the brushwood," lived in permanent shelters and raised corn to some extent. As they came in contact with both French traders and Spanish missionaries, they became less cannibalistic and better farmers. But they too lost numbers steadily, particularly during a smallpox epidemic. By the mid-nineteenth century only a handful survived in small villages near Montgomery, Texas. The early settlers found them peaceable and honest. Eventually the Bidais remnants intermarried with the neighboring Caddoes or other Atakapan bands in Louisiana and were seen no more in Texas.

Because the attention of Texas archeologists was drawn to campsites frequented by more aggressive tribes with richer cultures, almost no studies on the Atakapan Indians took place until the early 1950's, and then only in a small way. However, a large Indian mound, over one hundred feet square and six feet high, drew the attention of amateurs and then experts. It was located west of Houston in the Addicks Basin. A careful examination of the mound, which was made up of refuse and shells, yielded bone fragments, clamshells, pieces of turtle carapace, pottery shards, projectile points, flint knives and scrapers. Altogether nine campsites were located, and several graves. One skeleton uncovered lay on its right side, the arms folded in front of the chest with the hands to the chin and the legs pulled up against the pelvis. Intensive study of the artifacts indicated that these sites, now included in a so-called

Galveston Bay Focus or culture, had been abandoned at the end of the sixteenth century, before the people had been strongly influenced by either the Spanish or French. The remains are similar to those uncovered from another Atakapan "dig" on the Bolivar Peninsula. Some relics were given to the Smithsonian Institution in Washington, D.C., and others found their way into various county and state museums in Texas. Although it is well to know about these scavengers of the coast, the barbaric Atakapans are almost entirely overshadowed by their powerful and superior neighbors on the north, the Caddoes.

VI

The Caddo Confederacies

LONG BEFORE white men drew boundaries to parcel off the present states of Texas and Louisiana, various peoples wandered into the region between the upper Trinity River in Texas and the Mississippi River. Anthropologists cannot pinpoint their place of origin. As generations passed, some divided into separate tribes, some merged to form a new identity, and some vanished entirely.

Primarily they were farmers, and at an unknown date became mound builders. Since the rich soil yielded a bountiful supply of food, they had leisure time for developing a complex social organization and elaborate religious ceremonies. At the peak of their growth, those living along the Trinity and Red rivers were Texas' most productive and splendid people. We know them as the Caddoes. They were not a single tribe, but a large loosely-joined federation of some two dozen tribes. All spoke the Caddoan language.

The largest confederacy, comprising eight or nine tribes, was the Hasinai (or Asinai), who occupied the handsome valleys of the upper Neches and Angelina rivers. The Hasinai are of special interest, because the tribes of this confederacy called themselves *tayshas*, meaning "friends" or "allies." The Spaniards adopted the term but wrote it as *tejas* (tay-has). Over the years *tejas* finally became Texas. The Caddoes described in this chapter are Tejas.

A second confederacy, comprising four tribes, occupied the great bend of the Red River in northeastern Texas. Primarily they were lumped under the name of Kadohadachos. Still another Caddoan-speaking people were found near the Red River around the present Wichita Falls. They were Wichitas, discussed in the following chapter.

Archeologists state that before 500 A.D. several vigorous and successful peoples occupied the southland from the Trinity River eastward to the Atlantic Coast. When their population and wealth increased substantially, they could afford to pay hundreds of laborers to build large earthen temple mounds. Since little evidence of this highly developed culture survived in Texas, the experts can only guess by studying the remains of Louisiana sites how these Caddoan people lived. However, since the Tejas and others lived on the extreme westerly fringe of Caddo territory, their culture was less elaborate and their mounds modest when compared to more easterly developments.

By the time Luis de Moscoso and his armored soldiers moved through the Hasinai territory in 1542, the Tejas were past their prime. They had slipped back into a more primitive way of life, in spite of the fact that they lived in a region that abounded in resources. On the uplands of this gently rolling country were magnificent stands of loblolly, longleaf, and shortleaf pine trees. The fertile river bottomland produced bumper crops. Thickets abounded with black bear and deer, and plants that provided a rich store of nuts, seeds, and fruit.

Since their granaries and storage receptacles bulged with food, the Tejas had little inclination to make war on their neighbors, the Atakapans and Tonkawas. At the same time, they were powerful and numerous enough to discourage raids from those savages. Until the beginning of the seventeenth century the Tejas led a fairly peaceful existence. This is evidenced by the fact that their comfortable grass lodges were widely spaced, and the villages numbering two hundred or more families were impossible to defend.

Caddoan history, as written down by the Spaniards and French who encountered them in the seventeenth and eighteenth centuries, does not go back before the time when they were farmers. Scholars believe the Tejas came from a region near the confluence of the Red and Mississippi rivers. The Tejas said their people emerged from the underworld to the earth's surface. "First an old man climbed up, carrying in one hand fire and a pipe, and in the other a drum. Next came his wife with corn and pumpkin seeds."

The Europeans who first encountered them found their appearance startling because their heads were elongated, tapering off almost to a point at the top. This deformation was brought about by binding the infants' soft skulls with wooden shingles until the desired shape was attained. The Tejas tattooed their faces and bodies elaborately by scratching or pricking the skin until blood flowed, and rubbing powdered charcoal into the incisions. Both sexes punctured their ears and noses so they could wear ornaments of shells, bones, and colored stones. They wore jewelry at their ankles, knees, wrists, and necks. Some authorities claim the word "caddo" is derived from a Kiowa word meaning "pierced nose." Others say the origin of the name is not known, and it is not the one the people used to denote themselves.

Their deerskin clothing was little different from other Indians', except that it was superbly tanned to a glossy black color, was more neatly sewed, and was decorated with tiny white seeds, turkey feathers, and painted designs. Hair styles varied from tribe to tribe. The most widely used for men was a very short cropping of all the hair on the head except for a small patch on top, which grew waist-long and was adorned with feathers. In another style, all the hair was shaved off except for a narrow scalp lock extending from the forehead to the neck. Caddo women combed their hair and tied it at the nape of the neck with a strip of rabbitskin.

Most unusual, and unpleasant to white men's ears, was the Caddo custom of howling and weeping. The first Europeans to encounter the Tejas were startled at being welcomed with about a half hour of hideous yowling. Both sexes wept copiously in observing happy and sad occasions, and could stop the flow of tears quickly and go about their business. When they went visiting, they and their hosts observed a period of weeping at the time of arrival and departure.

Planting gardens, weeding, and harvesting were chores shared jointly but not equally by men and women. The men did the heavier tasks and left the routine drudgery to the women. Mostly corn, beans, squash, tobacco, and sunflowers (for seeds) were planted. Enough seed stock was preserved to ensure crops for the next two years. Planting was a communal affair, and a family's garden was put in according to its rank in Tejas society. That is, the leaders' plots were planted first, then those of the sub-officials, the middle class, and on down to the lowest of the servant class. Tools were crude, considering that the Tejas were an intelligent people. The principal one was the shoulder blade of a buffalo, bound onto a wooden shaft to form a hoe.

Corn was roasted or boiled, or pounded into flour for making a kind of bread and gruel. It was stored in large baskets.

Although the people relied primarily on crops, the men hunted bears for their fat, which was rendered out and stored in jars, and deer for their meat and skins. The meat was sliced thinly and dried on racks over a slow fire or in the sun. In addition, the men sought wild game birds, particularly prairie chickens, ducks, and wild turkeys.

One Caddo method of fishing is still being used. First, several short lines were tied to hooks, which were baited with rotten meat. Then these were attached to a long line, which was fastened to a tree at one end and weighted with sinkers at the other. This long line, called a trotline, was hauled in several times daily, the fish removed, and the hooks baited for another catch. The fish were preserved for future use by being smoked over a slow fire.

Tejas women were experts at tanning skins, at weaving mats and baskets, and at fashioning colorful pottery. The men fashioned a superior bow of Osage-orange wood, which was much in demand as a trade item.

Houses were small or large, depending on the owner's rank. Their construction was a communal affair. A family didn't just decide to build a house and select the site it liked best. First members asked permission to build from an official called a *caddi*. He selected the site, the date construction would start, and named lesser officials, called *tammas*, who chose the actual workmen. The latter were divided into four specialties: those who dug holes for the supporting poles, those who cut and hauled the poles to the site, those who set them in place, and those who put on the outer wall of matted grass. The *caddi* served as overseer. The *tammas* stood around with switches in hand to guarantee that the men and women laborers worked at a steady pace.

Meantime the family prepared a feast of boiled corn and

roast venison. When the house was completed, the officials were invited to eat. The *caddi* was fed first, then the *tammas*, and lastly, at a second sitting, the workers. No one received pay or gifts. House-raising was as social an occasion then as it was later, when white settlers came from miles around to help a newcomer raise his cabin.

The people's customs in rearing children, marriage, and burials did not differ enough from those of other Texas Indians to merit description. Their political organization, however, was extraordinary. The Hasinai confederacy operated as a bureaucracy. There were graded offices, duties, and ranks from the head man down to the humblest servant. The chief of the confederacy was called *xinesi*. His office was hereditary, and passed from father to son, or to the nearest male blood relation.

Next in rank were the *caddices*, or chiefs of the member tribes. They were assisted by *canhas*, but the fourth-ranking *chayas* actually carried out their orders. Below the *chayas* were the *tammas*, whom one scholar waggishly called the "sergeants."

The people functioned in kinship or clan units, which frequently placed their houses near one another, forming family hamlets within a village. The latter often numbered two hundred or more dwellings, and were separated by at least forty miles of river bottomland from each other.

The Tejas believed in one supreme deity or spirit who created the world, but they also revered other supernatural helpers. All were worshiped in temples, which were larger than the largest houses but of similar design. The floors were carpeted with reed mats, the altars made of wood and mats, and benches lined the walls. The fire burning in the center was

This drawing shows a Caddo chief in the mid-nineteenth century, long after the peak of the confederacies' strength.

never allowed to go out, and fires in family dwellings were lighted from it.

Near the temple was a sort of assembly house, used only when the tribal chieftan called his sub-officials into session. They were attended by young pages. Close by this house were two small structures supposedly occupied by the *coconicis*, or "spirit boys," who acted as intermediaries and oracles between the supreme deity and *xinesi*. When he wished to communicate with them, he called the lesser dignitaries to the temple. They sat about him in the darkness and listened as the *xinesi* spoke to the *coconicis* in his natural voice. Their answers were conveyed by the *xinesi* using an unnatural (and probably eerie) "spirit" voice. After the *coconicis* finished speaking, the *xinesi* resumed his natural voice to repeat their instructions to the officials. They, in turn, passed the word out to *tammas*, who told the families and workers. The instructions had to be carried out to the letter, or bad luck would befall the people.

The centuries-long peace which the Tejas enjoyed came to an end in the latter half of the seventeenth century, when hordes of southern-plains Apaches swooped down on one village after another, seeking loot and slaves. Being mounted, they had no difficulty defeating the horseless Caddoes. The men were cruelly slain and the villages burned, and the young women and children were taken across the Texas Panhandle and sold at Santa Fe, New Mexico.

This situation lessened after the Tejas allied with the Jumanos of the West Texas plains, who traded them horses for corn. By 1700 the Caddoes had learned to tighten their village plan and place their lodges on small plots behind log stockades. Meantime, the Apaches were occupied fighting the Wichitas and Comanches, so the raids almost ceased. Another threat, however, loomed on the Tejas' horizon.

In 1542, after three years of fruitless searching for gold northward from Florida to the Carolinas and westward into Tennessee and Arkansas, the Spanish expedition led by Hernando de Soto had paused to rest near the site of modern Natchez, Mississippi. Here De Soto died of a fever, and his remains were committed in a secret burial to the depths of the great river. When Luis de Moscoso assumed command of the survivors, he first led them westward into Texas in an attempt to reach Mexico. But the vastness of Caddo-land broke their spirit, and they trudged back to the Mississippi. They built boats, rowed down to the Gulf and across its blue expanse, and finally reached a Spanish settlement at Panuco, Mexico.

After that, nearly 150 years passed before the French explorer La Salle visited a neighboring tribe, the Nabedaches, in 1686. But neither the Spaniards nor the French had much impact on the Caddoes. A Spanish attempt to found a mission to serve them failed. A French trading post established on the south bank of the Red River in 1719 introduced the model of a stockaded post and the use of guns, which the French traded for corn. But after 1803, when the United States purchased the Louisiana Territory, Europeans largely withdrew from northeast Texas.

Still, the Caddoes did not regain the strength they had enjoyed before the Apaches decimated their ranks. The smallpox and syphilis, introduced by the Spaniards, ravaged the remaining villages, and by the 1830's, when Anglo-American settlers gazed avidly on their lush valleys, the dregs of this once-great people offered no resistance. As were other Texas Indians, they were engulfed in the tidal wave of American expansion.

In 1854 the federal government raked in the remnants of Caddo, Wichita, and Tonkawa Indians and corralled them on a small reservation along the Clear Fork of the Brazos River. But the peace and security they wanted so badly escaped them here, also. Comanche raids had infuriated the pioneer settlers so much that they wanted their state rid of all Indians, good or bad. The only solution that would safeguard the lives of the reservation Indians was to move them under military escort out of Texas onto the Wichita reservation near Anadarko, in western Oklahoma.

Although no longer harried by raids, the Caddoes lived in such abject poverty there that they lost many more people. But in 1902 every individual listed on a Caddo tribal role, which included Caddoes from as far north as Kansas, was given an allotment of land by the government and full citizenship. Less than 1200 were listed as remaining on the reservation in 1958. Presumably the rest had intermarried with other Indians or whites. Thus the Tejas lost forever their identity with Texas history.

VII

The Wichitas

MUCH HAS BEEN WRITTEN about the travels of the Spanish and French throughout Texas, and the migration of Americans and Germans to its grassy plains and meandering river bottoms. But little attention has been paid the long, roundabout movement of two Caddoan-speaking peoples from the lower reaches of the Red River up the west bank of the Mississippi and Missouri to the shallow muddy Platte River. At this point the two peoples apparently separated. One group, the Pawnees, adapted to life on the windy central plains of Nebraska. The other people, whom we know as the Wichitas, drifted down into the valleys of the Smoky Hill and middle Arkansas rivers in western Kansas. Their new home pleased them and by the mid-sixteenth century they had established more than twenty villages in the area.

In 1540 a large Spanish expedition led by Francisco Vásquez de Coronado wintered at the Pecos pueblo in New Mexico. The leader was avid for gold and glory, and thus easily duped by an Indian known as "the Turk," who claimed that far to the northeast was a province rich in gold and precious gems. The following spring he led Coronado across the buffalo plains of the Texas Panhandle in search of this province, which Coronado named Quivira. When it eluded him, the conquistador divided his force and sent part back to Mexico. He continued northward for more than a month, determined to find and plunder Quivira. But instead of discovering a glittering city where houses of alabaster were studded with jewels and the streets were paved with gold, Coronado found only a stinking village of grass huts inhabited by dark-skinned savages. This village was located at the great bend of the Arkansas. Coronado pushed on to the other villages, and found them no different from the first one. Bitterly disillusioned, ragged and half starved, he and the few who had not deserted or died along the way turned back to Mexico. The Turk paid dearly for misleading him.

Other Spanish expeditions visited the Indians whom Coronado named Quiviras, and were annihilated. The Quiviras, who were Wichitas, held sway in their realm for several generations until forced out. Powerful Osage war parties from the north and Comanche raiders rampaging down from the mountain-ringed headwaters of the Arkansas River overwhelmed one after another of their scattered, defenseless villages. Since the Wichitas had acquired a few horses by this time, the late seventeenth century, and knew more were available in the south, they slowly withdrew in that direction.

In present-day Oklahoma they were joined by the Tawakonis and Wacos, close cultural relatives who also spoke the Wichita language. The Wichitas settled on the south bank of the Red River, east of the site of Wichita Falls, Texas. The Wacos and Tawakonis ventured farther down through central Texas to the Brazos. All told the three major peoples and their sub-groups probably numbered about 2600 persons.

The first Spaniards who encountered the Wichitas along the Red River actually visited a sub-group, whom they called

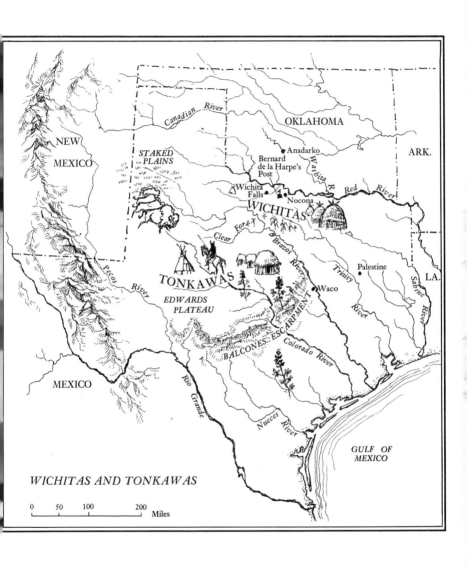

NEW
MEXICO

OKLAHOMA

ARK.

Canadian River

*STAKED
PLAINS*

• Anadarko

Bernard
de la Harpe's
Post

*Wichita
Falls*

• Nocona

WICHITAS

Washita R.

Red River

LA.

Pecos River

Clear Fork

TONKAWAS

Brazos River

Palestine •

*EDWARDS
PLATEAU*

• Waco

Trinity River

Sabine River

BALCONES ESCARPMENT

Colorado River

MEXICO

Rio Grande

Nueces River

**GULF OF
MEXICO**

WICHITAS AND TONKAWAS

0   50   100   200
                            Miles

Taovayas. The Wichitas proper, who lived in a separate village, were called Norteños, or Peoples or Nations of the North. Then, in 1719, Bernard de la Harpe, a French trader, established a stockaded post on the site of one of these villages. He armed the Indians, and quite possibly taught them new defensive tactics.

Europeans were not the only ones to appear among the Wichitas. The Comanches were taking over the West Texas plains from the Apaches, but they had learned that they couldn't fight everybody. In 1747 the Comanches negotiated a treaty with the Wichitas, which enabled them to bring their Apache prisoners and horses to the fort and trade them for French-manufactured guns and Wichita-grown crops.

In 1759 a Spanish expedition led by Colonel Diego Ortiz Parrilla found the Indians, but no French, entrenched behind the stoutly stockaded fort, which still flew the French flag. When Parrilla attacked the post, the Indians drove his force back so hard that they beat a hasty retreat and never returned. Gradually the post on the Red River fell into disuse. Today, anyone wishing to visit the site, which is seventeen miles out of Nocona in Montague County, will discover that it is called Old Spanish Fort. Nothing of the original structures remain. Oil-field and cattle-ranch operations now dominate the region between the Red and upper Brazos.

As mentioned earlier, the Tawakonis and Wacos had pushed farther southward and settled along the Brazos near present-day Waco, and along the upper Trinity near present-day Palestine, Texas. They adapted easily to a semi-plains-existence, based partly on agriculture but increasingly on buffalo hunting. White settlers who appeared in the 1850's were told by the Wacos that the Great Spirit had guided them to the fertile valley of the Brazos, promising that as long as the people drank from the gushing springs there, they would be strong and prosper. The white settlers appreciated the value of the springs, and soon evicted the Indians. Nowadays the springs are enclosed in a public park. A theater was built on the site of the Wacos' burial ground, and many a skull and artifact unearthed in the construction ended up in souvenir-collectors' hands.

The pioneer settlers found the Wichitas easy to distinguish from the Comanches, because their skin was darker and they practiced far more elaborate tattooing than the plains raiders. Wichita men tattooed their eyelids to such an extent that their name for themselves was something like "raccoon-eyed people." When a boy killed his first bird with a bow and arrow, the back of his hand was tattooed with the design of the bird's claw. Later, as he earned other honors in hunting or waging war against the Tonkawas, additional designs were cut into the flesh of his chest and upper arms. Like the Comanches and Apaches, the Wichita men pierced their ears so they could wear dangling ornaments. The women used facial and body paint as well as a tattooed line down the ridge of the nose, two lines around the mouth, and four vertical lines on the chin intersecting a single one along the chin line. They also tattooed small triangular designs on the arms, neck, and breasts.

Wichita villages were surrounded with cleared fields planted with corn, beans, and pumpkins. Weeds were chopped out, but no form of irrigation was employed even when a plentiful supply of water was close at hand. Oddly enough, the people did not eat fish. They supplemented their diet with buffalo meat and fresh wild plums.

Their dwellings followed the Caddo pattern of being circular, with forked poles supporting walls made of bound clumps of grass. At the top, where the poles came together, the women placed a bundle of grass in which was inserted four short sticks. The bundle represented the Great Spirit, and the sticks pointed in the four directions, or quarters, in which the creator divided the world. Small doors made of grass tied to a willow frame opened on the east and west. The houses were raised with as much ceremony as that of their eastern neighbors, the Tejas.

The Wichita social organization was based on the matrilinear system. Thus a family was composed of a mature woman who was considered "the mother," plus her husband, unmarried children, married daughters and their families, and her sisters and their families. As the anthropologist W. W. Newcomb states, this was the basic economic unit of Wichita life. If the older woman died, her position was taken by her oldest daughter. The family was the strongest social unit, and next to it, the village. There was no strong central tribal organization. Each village had its chief, or a first and second chief, chosen by a council of warriors. If there were two chiefs, one devoted himself to civil matters and the other acted as a war chief.

Although Wichita life was not geared intensively to breeding warriors and waging war, as was that of the Comanches and Apaches, Wichita men were never loath to organize a raiding party and go for scalps, captives, and horses. Any warrior who had proved himself had no difficulty in leading a raiding party. One factor resulting in the eventual downfall of the Wichitas was their preference for warring in small parties, rather than coming together to fight in large numbers under the command of an outstanding military leader.

Wichita belief in the supernatural was unique in that the people worshiped several gods, some male, some female. The creator of the universe, or supreme power, was called *Kinni-*

Wichita dwellings were made of forked poles, covered with clumps of grass; in later times some huts were fitted with wooden doors.

kasus. Next came the sun god, whose name meant Man-Reflecting-Light. Morning Star, spirit of the first man on earth, brought daylight. North Star, or Light-Which-Stands-Still, was created to help men orient themselves while on earth. Moon, or Bright-Shining-Woman, was the wife of North Star. She was also the first woman created and therefore mother of the human race. Another female deity was Woman-Having-Powers-In-The-Water, who provided water for drinking, washing, and growing crops. In contrast to the Christian belief, Wichita believed that everything on earth—living or not—possessed a spirit or soul. They also believed in an after-life, but happiness there depended on the good and bad the person had done while on earth. There were a number of religious ceremonies that took the form of dances and singing. Some were directed toward deities and some were seasonal celebrations. Each ceremony was directed by a separate society devoted to its proper observance and perpetuation of its traditions.

When white settlers displaced the Wichitas and forced them into Comanche territory, the people found themselves attacked by whites, Comanches, and their long-time enemies, the Tonkawas. By 1859 their situation was so desperate that they willingly withdrew to a federal reservation set aside for Wichitas, Tawakonis, Wacos, and other sub-groups near Anadarko, Oklahoma.

VIII

The Tonkawas

Two HUNDRED YEARS AGO, if you could have asked a Comanche warrior what he thought of the Tonkawa Indians, he
would have pantomined extreme loathing and spat out the
tribal epithet for "cannibal." Yet the label of cannibalism, so
widely associated with the people who roamed the hill country of central Texas, is somewhat misleading. Primarily the
Tonkawas were a peace-loving people and one of the few who
were friendly to the early white settlers. If attacked by their
enemies, the Karankawas and later the Comanches, they
fought like cornered wildcats. When they killed an enemy,
consuming bits of his flesh was largely a ritualistic practice accompanied by dancing and singing. Supposedly the act enabled the Tonkawas to acquire some of their victim's power
and courage. At the same time it destroyed his spirit, and in-
sulted those who had failed to protect his body.

Because of the pioneers' deep-seated mistrust of any Indians and the language barrier, they gained little first-hand
knowledge of Tonkawa culture. Thus when Noah Smithwick
or John Jenkins witnessed acts of cannibalism and described
them in revolting detail, they interpreted the deeds only from
their own civilized viewpoint. They saw them only as acts of

unspeakable savagery, completely devoid of any spiritual or ritualistic meaning. But after anthropologists learned something of the Tonkawas' spirit-ridden existence, they viewed their cannibalism with more than just disgust. They could appreciate why the people acted with savage delight when able to "borrow" courage from an enemy's spirit, and at the same time show contempt for it and insult his family. Since the Tonkawas never were militarily strong, they suffered greatly from enemy raids. There were few opportunities to celebrate a victory by eating enemy flesh. Perhaps this is why the people exploded so savagely when the occasion did arise.

The tribal name, Tonkawa, was derived from a Waco word that meant "they all stay together." However, the Tonkawas' name for themselves was *tickanwatic*. This had a slightly different meaning, which implied that, at least among themselves, the Tonkawas were "the most human of people." The tribe was made up of countless small bands and sub-groups, some of which actually were family clans. Each was self-governing and ruled by a chief. Not until after repeated attacks from the Comanches and the pressures and diseases introduced by white settlers had made life too dangerous for separate bands did the misery-ridden remnants form a single and somewhat stronger tribe.

Some experts link the Tonkawas to the Coahuiltecans who lived to the south, and relate their language to the Coahuiltecan linguistic stock. The principal bands included the Mayeye, Yojaune, Ervipiame, Cavas or Lavas, Emet, Tohaha, Toho, and Sana. Cabeza de Vaca might have encountered one of these in his wanderings. An account of the Alonso de León expedition of 1690 states that when the Spaniards came into view, the Tonkawas "made for the wood, leaving to us the *ranchería*, together with the laden dogs, which they had not been able to drive fast enough when they fled." These were thought to be Emets or Cavas. Obviously the Tonkawas had not yet acquired horses, since they were still following the age-old custom of plains Indians in using dogs as beasts of burden.

The original range of the Tonkawas was the vast sunny expanse of the Edwards Plateau, which rises in giant steps from the coastal plain and dominates the south-central portion of the state. Since the altitude varies from one to three thousand feet above sea level, the Tonkawas experienced less enervating heat and malarial fevers than their coastal neighbors. The plateau was watered by some twelve rivers, which were fed by small creeks and cold burbling springs. The people camped in the narrow green valleys where modern cattle and dude ranches now prevail. In March, literally hundreds of acres of the heavenly bluebonnet burst into bloom. The Spaniards called it buffalo clover or *el conejo*, the rabbit, because the white tip of the flower resembled a rabbit's tail. But after white women arrived, they thought the shape of the blue flower was like the calico sunbonnets they wore to protect their fair skin from the Texas sun, and they named it the blue-bonnet. In 1901 their descendants brought about its selection as the state flower of Texas.

Since the plateau was overrun with buffalo, the Tonkawas geared their lives to the movements of the herds. However, where the Comanches and Kiowas and the Sioux and Crow were able to enrich their culture by adapting to a plains existence, the Tonkawas remained a primitive and unattractive people. They had little to distinguish them from other native Texas Indians. They wore as little clothing as possible in warm weather, and the usual shirts, skirts, robes, and moccasins when it was cold. Both men and women tattooed and painted their faces and the upper portions of their bodies. The men wore their hair long, either hanging loosely or plaited in braids. When a young man had proved himself as a warrior, he wore a headdress of feathers and buffalo horns on special occasions, or whenever he felt like showing off. The designs and colors he adopted in applying face and body paint were symbolical of his deeds and of the messages he received from his personal spirits. Thus a design was his alone, and no other warrior could copy it without his permission.

Tonkawa weapons were the usual bow and arrow, lance, and war club. None were really well made. The men hunted buffalo, deer, rabbits, skunks, rats, and land tortoises. The women dried the meat that was not eaten immediately, and added roots, fruits, seeds, and nuts to the family larder. Since they were a nomadic hunting people, the families built thatched lodges in their villages but used portable tepees while hunting. The latter were smaller and far less attractive than the handsome painted tepees of the conquering Comanches. The women did not bother making pottery, because it was traded from the friendly Caddoan-speaking Tejas.

Before the Comanches brought an end to this trade, the Tejas journeyed every year to the land of the Tonkawas. They traded their pottery, corn, and bows for buffalo and deer hides and flint points. The Tonkawas "mined" these cherished flints from the steep rocky face of the Balcones Escarpment, which formed much of the southern and eastern boundaries of the Edwards Plateau. When a runner brought word that the Tejas were approaching, the Tonkawas put on their best clothes and went out to greet them. The guests were entertained with feasts and dancing and an exchange of gifts. The chiefs and warriors renewed their pledges of friendship and agreed to help each other beat off Apache and, later, Comanche raids.

Each Tonkawa clan adopted a name to distinguish its members from others. These names were taken from animals such as the wolf or buffalo, or from plants, reptiles, and even physical characteristics such as "mouth-open people." The clans were matrilineal in organization. A newly married couple lived with the wife's clan. Thus, children were born into their mother's clan rather than their father's. This also held true of grandchildren. The clan was a very closely knit group. If parents were separated or died, their children were cared for by their grandmothers and aunts. When a father died, his property was left to the clan, not his children, so that when his sons married, they could not take their share from their clan to enrich another.

Apparently some clans held festivals in honor of their "name" animal. For instance, in his splendid book titled *Indians of the Southwest*, M. Jourdan Atkinson described a Wolf dance celebrated by members of the Wolf clan. The men, clad in skins of the timber wolf, gathered after dark under a brush arbor. They sat on their haunches and bayed at the moon. Later they circled, snuffing, scratching, twitching tied-on tails, and snapping at each other as wolves do. All this was done to the beat of a drum. When the beat quickened, they turned to digging with their "paws," faster and faster, like dogs unearthing a bone.

At length, they uncovered a man who emerged slowly from the ground, and shrugged off the dirt clinging to his body. This episode symbolized the origin of the first Tonkawan. Before the ceremony began, the man had been buried with a hollow reed in his mouth, through which he sucked air. After he emerged, he made a speech, saying that now he had appeared on earth, he didn't know what to do. The "wolves" withdrew to "talk," with much snapping and growling, and returned to present him a bow and arrow. Then the spokesman said, "Go now. Fight as we do. Take what you need and kill what you will, for you are armed." The man then thanked the donors politely, whereupon the "wolves" threw off their skins and joined him in a joyful celebration.

Instead of despising the Tonkawas, the pioneer settlers should have sought vaulable information from them about animals, plants, and the weather. Time after time their cattle were drowned when storms in the headwaters country turned gentle rivers into raging flash floods. A Tonkawa could have told them to take note if crickets ceased to sing suddenly and it became very still. That was the time to "hurry, hurry" and move the cattle and goods out of the lowlands, because the water was coming down.

Little is known of the rules that governed birth, rearing children, and marriage. Death, rather than birth or marriage, seems to have been the event celebrated with the most elaborate ceremonies. When an ailing individual was about to die, his relatives and friends gathered in his tepee. Some sat in a circle about him, and placed their hands on his body. Others formed a second, or a third circle, placing their hands on the shoulders of those in front of them. For hours they chanted and swayed in the murky firelight. When death came, the mourners moved to the grave site. The body was prepared immediately for burial by cutting the hair, painting the face yellow, and wrapping the remains in a buffalo robe. If all the taboos were observed, the dead person's spirit would travel swiftly to its new home in the western sky. For four days the women wailed and tore their hair. Then the chief announced that the deceased's name must never again be used. After the

Members of the Wolf clan celebrated the origin of the Tonkawa in an elaborate dance.

medicine man conducted a purification ceremony for those contaminated by their closeness to the deceased, family life resumed its normal pattern.

The spirits of the dead had an abnormally strong influence on the well-being of every family. No doubt about it, the Tonkawas were a haunted people. If one or more taboos had been broken, the spirits of dead men hovered around, waiting to frighten the relatives or cause trouble. Every strange sound created by the wind or a creaking tree trunk or gurgling stream was thought to be the voice of an unhappy spirit whose body had not been prepared properly for burial. Perhaps it had not been placed in the proper position in the grave, with the feet toward the east. Maybe the cherished belongings had been kept by niggardly relatives instead of being placed on the grave. Or maybe the ashes of the dead man's pipe had not been hidden, or his favorite horse or dog had not been slain atop the grave. Possibly the relatives had eaten between the time of death and the final burial rites. Maybe, without thinking, some one had spoken the dead person's name aloud. This was the worst offense of all, yet very difficult to avoid. There were many other taboos also. Small wonder that few Tonkawa families could escape violating one or more, and thus were haunted by restless unhappy spirits.

The Tonkawas served Sam Houston well enough as scouts, before and after the battle of San Jacinto, to merit his official and public praise. Later they helped the Texas militia track down Comanche raiders. For this they paid dearly. The Comanches swarmed over them like vengeful hornets, and the whites ignored their cries for help. The casualties suffered then and from a severe smallpox epidemic reduced their population to a few hundred souls.

In the 1850's the federal government moved the remnants

onto a reservation on the Clear Fork of the Brazos. When the Texans demanded that all Indians be expelled from the state, the Tonkawas were moved to another reserve along the Washita River in southwestern Oklahoma. These families gradually died out or married with those of other tribes. To-day there are no Tonkawas listed in the latest census of Indians living on reservations.

PART TWO
The Comanches

Check-Out Receipt

Alameda Free Library
Main Branch
1550 Oak Street
Alameda, CA 94501
Tel: 510-747-7777
www.alamedafree.org
Checkout Date: 02-19-2015 - 16:10:24

Patron ID.: xxxxxxxxxx8867

---

1 Comanches And Other Indians Of Texas
33341000130335   DueDate: 03/12/15

Total Items: 1

Balance Due: $ 0.00

Libraries now closing at 5:00 p.m.
on Thursdays.

IX

The Comanche People

FAR NORTH OF TEXAS, in prehistoric times, small bands of Sho-
shonean-speaking people roamed across the Wyoming plains
and the great interior basin west of the Rocky Mountains.
Finding enough to eat took so much time and effort that the
people had little energy left for improving their crude tools or
enriching their way of life, but about 1700 these people,
whom we know as the Comanches, obtained their first horses.
Possibly they got them through trade with other tribes who,
in turn, acquired them by barter or theft from the markets at
Santa Fe, New Mexico. To a hungry people, horses must have
been welcomed as a generous source of meat and hides, or as
pack animals able to transport heavier loads than the women
or dogs. But when the traders taught them how to handle the
animals to greater advantage in hunting and waging war, they
sought them avidly. As the animals increased from a few
scrubby mustangs to herds numbering thousands, the weak,
impoverished people acquired food aplenty and "walking
wealth," as horses were called.

Walter Prescott Webb, famed Texas historian, wrote,
"Steam, electricity, and gasoline have wrought no greater
changes in our culture that did horses in the culture of the

Soon after 1700, horses became a vital part of the Comanche culture.

Plains Indians." This was especially true of the Comanches. Not only did possession of horses enrich their culture and vocabulary; it changed the character of the people. Once mounted, the men blossomed into superb cavalrymen and vicious raiders. Fighting and pillaging became the central focus of their existence. They struck off from their Shoshone homeland and moved south. By 1705 they were terrorizing the natives of the southwest, and had swept eastward onto the open grasslands. Their savage exploits earned them the reputation of being "lords of the plains."

Since the Comanches were the Indians most widely encountered by the Anglo-American settlers in Texas, they will be described in greater detail than those peoples who had almost become extinct, or whose way of life had deteriorated before the Texas pioneers came onto the scene. Much has been written about the struggle of the Spaniards, French, Mexicans, and pioneering Anglo-Americans for possession of Texas. Yet more lives were lost, more captives taken, and more property stolen or destroyed in the decades of warfare during the nineteenth century waged by the Comanches and settlers against each other.

The tribal name is derived from a Ute word, *Komantcía,* meaning "enemy" or "anyone who wants to fight me all the time." No better name could have applied to this tribe. Comanches were indeed enemies, not only to the settlers but to the Wichitas, Tonkawas, and Lipan Apaches whom they drove out of West Texas.

By 1830 the Comanches numbered between fifteen and twenty thousand people, divided among a dozen or more tribes. They ranged through western and southern Kansas, eastern New Mexico, west and central Texas, and western Oklahoma. They never developed a strong central organization, because each tribe-within-the-tribe, or band or sub-group, jealously guarded its independence. Since there was a bewildering complex of these, only those best known in Texas history will be named here. Simplified names of the major sub-divisions include the Antelope or Quahadi (also spelled Kwahadi), who controlled the Staked Plains; the Buffalo-eaters, whose favorite haunt was the valley of the Canadian River; the Nokoni, Tanima, and Tenawa, or Wanderers, who roamed from the Red River to the Brazos; the Penateka, or southern Comanches, also called the Honey-eaters or Wasps. They extended from the Cross Timbers belt in East Texas to the headwaters of the Brazos and Colorado rivers, and as far west as the Pecos. Sometimes the Wasps were called the Quick-stingers, a name meaning swift and deadly raiders.

Comanchería, as the realm of the Comanches was called, encompassed a vast area approximately six hundred miles long from north to south, and four hundred miles from east to west. Much of this sunny open land was level, or gently roll-ing, and cut by low-banked, sand-filled streams. However, the headwaters country of each stream was riddled with canyons and desolate "breaks," where campsites with sufficient water, wood, and grass were scarce.

Settlers described the Comanches as ordinary-looking, unattractive, slovenly people, who tended to put on weight as they aged. They had no outstanding physical characteristics, perhaps because they intermarried with their Indian, Mexican, and American captives. However, Comanches seen in camp, wearing only breechclouts or skirts and no face paint, were a far cry from Comanches dressed for special occasions. Then their outfits were lavishly ornamented with fringe, beads, and shiny bits of tin acquired in trade.

The women and girls wore buckskin skirts, loose-fitting

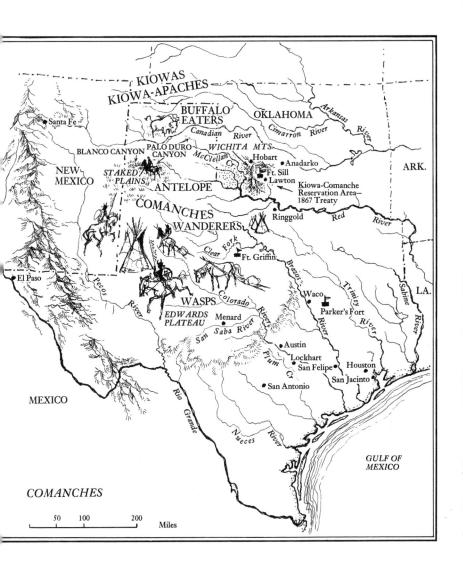

KIOWAS
KIOWA-APACHES

BUFFALO
EATERS   OKLAHOMA   Arkansas
                                        River
Santa Fe   Canadian   River   Cimarron   River

BLANCO CANYON   PALO DURO   WICHITA MTS.
                CANYON   McClellan   Hobart
NEW   Cr.   • Anadarko   ARK.
MEXICO   STAKED   Ft. Sill
         PLAINS   ANTELOPE   Lawton
                                        Kiowa-Comanche
              COMANCHES   Reservation Area—
              WANDERERS   1867 Treaty
                          Ringgold   Red   River

                    Clear Fork
                          • Ft. Griffin

El Paso   Brazos

              Pecos   Colorado   Waco

                    WASPS   Parker's Fort   Trinity
              EDWARDS   Menard
              PLATEAU   San Saba River   River

                          Plum   • Austin   Sabine   LA.
                          Cr.   • Lockhart
                              San Felipe   • Houston
                          • San Antonio   San Jacinto

MEXICO   Rio Grande

                    Nueces   River

                                   GULF OF
                                   MEXICO

COMANCHES

    50   100   200
|—|—|————|————————| Miles

blouses, and moccasins. They cropped their hair and painted their faces with red or yellow lines and dots about the eyes and cheeks. The men and boys wore fringed and beaded shirts and leggings. In cold weather both sexes donned overshoes of buffalo hide and superbly tanned robes.

The men were far more vain than the women. They spent hours plucking every hair from their faces and eyebrows with bone tweezers, and combing, greasing, and plaiting their long braids. Some spliced horsehair into them so they would reach to the ground. They were bound off with strips of fur or bright cloth. Pieces of glass, beads, metal, and single black or yellow feathers were attached to the side locks. The men favored necklaces of bears' claws, and beaded or copper wire bands to protect their left wrists from the painful sting of the bow string. But most of all they cherished earrings. During their teens the boys had their ears pierced by a woman who jabbed six to eight holes along the helix, or curved border of the upper external ear. A greased straw was set in the punctures until they healed. The favorite earrings were long, thin shells obtained from the Mexicans, silver or brass wire bangles, or even coins. Often their weight bent over the top of the ear, but the discomfort was borne gladly for the sake of vanity.

Face paint followed no set design. Members of one band did not paint similarly to differentiate themselves from others. Usually the center part of the hair was daubed with red, white, or yellow paint, and the face and ears with all sorts of scrolls, lines, triangles, and circles. Some painted half the face and chest in one color, half in another. Until late in the nineteenth century headdresses sported buffalo horns or deer antlers. These were attached to skull caps fringed with drooping feathers. Although some warriors later adopted long, lavish, feathered war bonnets, they never were as important to the Comanches as to the northern-plains tribes.

The Comanches enjoyed a bountiful supply of food. Millions of buffalo roamed throughout their land, and elk, deer, antelope, and bear were plentiful in the river valleys. There were seasonal crops of nuts, berries, and roots. The people liked corn and tobacco but satisfied their needs by trade or theft rather than tedious farming. Raiding parties took along extra ponies to be butchered as needed. While the warriors were fond of their war ponies, they had no qualms about eating horseflesh, or abusing or riding to death animals that displeased them. Dogs doubled as pets or watchdogs, as beasts of burden for transporting light packing cases, and, if necessity demanded, as stew meat.

Since the Comanches were nomads, everything they possessed had to be portable. Thus they favored the tepee, or conical skin dwelling. Like the Shoshones, Utes, Crows, and Blackfeet, the Comanche women used four long straight poles in the foundation framework. These were tied together at the top and set up, evenly spaced, in a circle. Next eighteen more poles were set in for strength. Then ten to seventeen buffalo hides, fitted and sewed together, were laid on until the walls were formed. A woman standing on another's shoulders fastened the coverings at the top. One skin fastened to a pole was only partially attached to the tepee so it could be laid back to open a smoke hole when needed. Within fifteen to twenty minutes the tepee was ready for use.

Most averaged twelve to fifteen feet in diameter at floor level, and comfortably sheltered ten to twenty members of a family. The door always faced the east, and was made of a stiff pelt fastened at the top and weighted at the bottom. The owner's bed was placed on the far side opposite the door, and those of his wives and children ranged on each side. The place of honor given a guest was the bed or seat to the immediate left of the owner. The robes were soft and warm, but infested with lice and fleas. Pillows were fashioned from small pelts and stuffed with grass. Back rests afforded comfortable lounging. In cold weather the walls were staked to the ground, but in warm weather they were raised several inches to provide ventilation. When storms raked the plains, additional skins were hung inside to stop floor drafts.

A Comanche camp ordinarily extended a mile or more along a stream, so each family would have grass enough at hand for their horses. By modern standards a village was far from clean, but by Indian standards Comanche tepees and their inhabitants were cleaner than most.

Every tepee had a shallow fire pit in the center. Only a small fire was needed for warmth. During the summer and autumn, the women cooked outside in the shade of a brush arbor. In the early days the Comanches used primitive hand drills to start their fires. After they obtained flints and steel from the Mexicans, they preferred this quicker method. Firewood was plentiful along the streams. On the treeless plains there was an inexhaustible supply of dried buffalo droppings, called chips, which provided a slow, long-lasting fire. In moving camp the tepee was dismantled, and the poles and hides were transported on travois. These were made of buffalo hides suspended between two lodge poles to form a platform or carrier. The weighted ends dragged on the ground, the middle part of the poles was supported by saddle loops, and the ends were tied together above the horse's neck. All other family possessions were stuffed in rawhide cases and carried either on additional travois or pack animals.

When Anglo-American settlers appeared in what is now Texas, the Comanches were so numerous that the name "Comanche" became synonymous with "Indian." They had developed a rich way of life little known to the whites, who lived in dread of their savagery.

X

From Birth to Burial

OFTEN WHEN a Comanche infant was born, the medicine woman attending the mother painted a black spot on the door of the family tepee. Thus the villagers learned that another child had arrived to strengthen the people. For a few days the newborn was watched over carefully, particularly if it was a healthy boy. If deformed, it was literally thrown away.

When the mother resumed her housekeeping duties, the child was swathed in soft buckskin and laced into a cradle board. There it remained, bodily restricted, wet and messy, during the daylight hours. Toward evening it was bathed and oiled, and even powdered with the pulverized dry rot of a cottonwood tree. Afterwards it was placed in a stiff rawhide tube, so it could sleep between the parents without being smothered.

While the mother worked, the cradle board was propped against the tepee or suspended from a tree trunk, or if the family was on the move, was hung on the mother's saddle. When about nine months old, the infant was allowed to creep about the tepee. Otherwise it was carried in a sling on the mother's back. There it was warm and comfortable, and happily secure. The child had a pet name but later on, at no certain age, the father or medicine man or woman provided a formal name. In a simple naming ceremony, the father lighted his stone pipe, and after blowing puffs of smoke toward heaven, earth, and the four winds, intoned a prayer. Then he held the child high, to symbolize the hope that it would grow up, and announced, "His [her] name is going to be . . ." If a boy was puny, the father asked a brave warrior to give it a strong name, such as He-Runs-Against-The-Enemy.

A Comanche child had many teachers, who taught gently, patiently, and repeatedly rules of behavior that were to his benefit. Constantly he was urged to emulate the skills or prowess of outstanding members of the band. He was not coaxed to be good, or frightened by threats of physical punishment. Rather, he was taught that the respect of his family and fellow tribesmen was most desirable, and their disapproval to be avoided.

When six years old, girls began learning household tasks and boys to hunt. Since both grew up with horses, they already had learned to ride, more by trial and error than formal instruction. All lessons brought the children into closer relationship with their parents. But grandparents had a very important role, too, instructing the young ones in tribal history, traditions, legends, religion, and taboos. If a grandchild was naughty, a grandfather might hide behind a robe in a shadowy place, cover his head with a whitened elkskin, and scare the youngster with ghostly mutterings. And all children shivered when warned that if they misbehaved, the Big Cannibal Owl, a mythological creature, would come out of his cave and eat them up!

Pre-adolescent boys and girls played in mixed groups. They enjoyed hide-and-seek, races on foot and horseback, and ball games. A favorite game was called "grizzly bear." A mound of sand called "the sugar" was piled up, and a child dragged around to smooth a circle about it. Next the players formed a line facing the circle, with hands on each other's waists. The leader was called "the mother," and protected her "children," the other players, from "the grizzly," who was "it" inside the circle. The "grizzly" tried to catch a child, as the line swung back and forth out of reach. When one' was caught, it was tickled or "eaten" by the "grizzly." While this was going on, the other players raced to steal some "sugar" without being caught. The game ended after all the "sugar" was stolen or all the players captured.

On rainy days the children huddled inside the tepees, because they and their parents were afraid of the fearsome spirits that were lightning and thunder. During winter storms or intense cold, they huddled around the fire, listening to stories.

As boys and girls entered their teens, they stopped playing together. The girls assumed more household tasks and began to act modestly and docilely, as was necessary if they hoped to attract a husband. The boys spent their time almost exclusively with men, learning to become hunters and warriors.

A boy really had the best of everything. He didn't have to do any chores other than learn to watch the pony herd, because the elders felt his time was better spent learning a man's skills. He was overindulged in many ways, because, as one medicine woman said, "he is going to be a warrior, and he may die young in battle." Playing in gangs was the teen-agers' way of life. One of the first things boys sought at a new campsite was a good swimming hole and a ballground. They wrestled and raced competitively, and played earnest war games identical to the "soldiers and Injuns" games of white youngsters in the frontier country. Of course in the Indian version, the Comanches came out winners!

Since knowing how to rope, break, train, and ride horses was absolutely essential, a boy spent many waking hours at these tasks and, in addition, at making his riding gear. Although the older men were the experts, the young person was expected to know how to do everything connected with horsemanship. The boys learned to steal horses by practicing on animals belonging to their families and friends. First they were taught to approach with extreme care from a downwind position so the horses would not get their scent. Then two or three would wrap in buffalo robes, sneak up on the herd after dark, and cut loose as many horses as they wanted, or as many as they could before a dog barked or a sentry shouted a warning. Time after time they did this, until they had "stolen" enough horses so that their warrior relatives were not left enough mounts to pursue them. Then at daylight they would ride back into camp, laughing and bragging, and receive the congratulations of the people.

Much was made of a boy's first buffalo kill, because the youth could not take part in a raid or fight until after he had killed one of the beasts. He must do this while riding full tilt in pursuit of the animal, either shooting arrows or driving a lance into its heart or lungs. Since this took considerable strength, skill, and daring, it helped prove a teen-ager was fit to accompany a raiding party. Then, if he acquitted himself well in a raid and brought back horses and other plunder, and particularly if he lifted a scalp, his father held a Give-Away Dance in his honor. At this affair, the father gave away blankets and horses so generously that sometimes the family became poverty-stricken. But it would gain back many items when other proud fathers held similar ceremonies. (When Comanche men returned home after fighting in World War II, they were honored as returning warriors with such dances.)

After a young man achieved the rank of warrior, either he or his parents arranged his marriage by calling on the chosen girl's father. They agreed on the number of horses which must be paid before she became his bride. Often the suitor had stolen enough horses so that he could marry a girl of his own choosing. But if he was poor, and he and the girl were very much in love, they could elope. Then the boy's family presented the girl's father with as many gifts as possible, so neither family would feel dishonored. A girl's family never sought a husband for her. That was considered disgraceful. If a girl couldn't get a husband, however, her father might ask an industrious captive to marry her and join the family.

The more famous and rich a warrior became, the more wives he could afford. Most seemed to limit themselves to three or four. It was not unusual for husbands to marry their wives' sisters. A woman whose husband died usually married his brother or a close relative. Marriages preferably took place between the families of one band, but there were no restrictions against marrying into others. One rule, which white families might have found beneficial, was that the members of a family *had* to get along, particularly the women. Also, a son-in-law had to respect his mother-in-law. If he didn't, she could order her daughter to leave him.

The first wife was the "chief" wife, and was boss over other wives or captive women, who served as "chore wives." The latter were welcomed by the chief wife because they saved her much drudgery. A wife acquired a tepee of her own after she had had children, and was expected to accept additional wives and their offspring.

Within a band or neighboring groups there was much visiting, feasting, dancing, and competitive sports. The Comanches were a very sociable people, and until the white man introduced intoxicating liquor, their gatherings were notable for the absence of drunkenness. The women, garbed in their best attire, formed teams of ten to play shinny or double ball, or kick-the-ball. The men preferred horse racing and marksmanship contests, and did not play lacrosse, as did most eastern tribes.

In good weather or bad, dice games played with pebbles or blocks of wood and other gambling games were extremely popular. Comanches did not disapprove of gambling, and tended to be extravagant in their wagers. Husbands and wives were free to gamble the family's possessions. If they lost, there was no trouble, because the Comanches considered paying gambling debts the same as giving gifts. Personal belongings changed hands so frequently that the people never coveted one another's property, and theft was unheard of.

Although bands and family groups might meet once a year for a communal buffalo hunt, the Comanches never did journey long distances in order to meet for a single great tribal ceremony or rendezvous. They did not feel impelled to come together as a people, as Kiowas did for their Sun Dance or Nez Percés at camass-bulb digging time. The cooperative buffalo hunts took place in the summer or late fall, when the hides were best. Each group sent a small delegation of head men to decide on the time and location. The decisions depended on the location of the nearest herd. Next, runners went out to locate the site for the temporary hunting camp, which had to be near water and wood. They marked the place by erecting many racks for drying the meat. Usually only the strong adults and teen-agers took part. The women drove pack animals loaded with utensils, skins for temporary shelters, and tools. The herders drove surplus pack ponies needed to carry meat and hides back to the villages. When all were settled at the new camp, the people staged a Hunting Dance. They wore their everyday clothes, since the dance had no spiritual significance and was purely an expression of joy.

The next day a respected warrior was named the hunt leader. He planned every detail. Since all the hunters charged the herd simultaneously, only the leader gave the signal to begin the attack. The Comanches were far more relaxed and informal in their hunt arrangements than the Cheyennes or Crows, who operated according to strict rules and under the surveillance of their military police.

Since the herd had already been spotted, the hunters moved out before dawn on their specially trained, fast hunting horses. They approached the herd downwind as quietly as possible. Then they dismounted briefly to strip down to their breechclouts and moccasins. They would ride bareback, controlling their mounts with knee pressure and commands so that their hands were free for shooting. With great caution they encircled the herd. On signal, the hunters began running around the herd, forcing the buffalo to close ranks. Cows and calves gathered in the center while the bulls milled around them, their broad flanks easy targets for the expert bowmen. As animal after animal toppled over, often the others became bewildered and ceased running. Killing them was easy, too. Often within an hour all the yowling, snorting, racket of pounding hooves and swirling dust had faded, and the plain was littered with the carcasses of many buffalo. However, unless the hunters were extremely fortunate, there always were casualties. Hunters had been thrown from their mounts, and some horses had broken a leg or had been gored by wounded bulls.

Each downed buffalo belonged to the hunter who had killed it. This was easily settled, because each hunter's arrows were distinctive. If a carcass bristled with several, the owner of the arrow (or lance) that had pierced the heart or lungs was given possession.

After time to relax and brag, the men took on the heavy grisly work of skinning and butchering. When the meat and hides were packed back to camp, the women's work began. They sliced the meat for quick drying in the sun, and pegged the hides, flesh side up, so that they could be scraped for tanning. In addition they cut off the wooly hair, horns, hooves, and bones for future use.

Hunting continued day after day until all the buffalo in the area had been killed and the families had enough food and robes for their major needs. After another feast and dance all returned to their villages.

As late as the 1830's buffalo was found as far south as Houston. But as whites moved onto the Texas plains, they either killed or drove off thousands of the animals so that the native grass could be grazed by their cattle and horses. By the 1840's buffalo were rare in East Texas, and thinning out in the central plains. While this posed problems for the Comanches, it did not worry them. They felt there would always be enough buffalo to sustain them. Thirty years later, white hide-hunters had shot the multi-million-head southern herd out of existence. Yet the Comanches stubbornly refused to believe the lumbering beasts were gone forever.

When the hunting parties returned to their families, they were honored with much feasting and dancing, and exchange of news. Those who stayed at home listened eagerly as the hunters bragged about their exploits. If some old fellow wished to tell about his accomplishments in bygone days, no matter how boring or long-winded he was, his audience listened politely. But finally everyone was talked out, and life resumed its post-hunt routine.

The plentiful supply of buffalo on the Texas plains provided Comanche families with hides for covering their tepees, buffalo robes, and much of their food.

The old men no longer able to hunt or fight gathered daily in a special tepee called a Smoke Lodge. Here, with great formality, they smoked and talked of past days of glory. Since there were always tasks for older women to perform, they never enjoyed such leisure. When an elderly person became helpless and was about to die, he was "thrown away." This custom was not as callous as it may seem. The old one formally disposed of his personal belongings and retired to a separate small lodge to be tended until death came. He voluntarily left the family lodge so that his ghost would not haunt the relatives.

Burial usually took place quickly after death. The body was washed and dressed in the best clothing, the eyelids were painted red and sealed with clay. The knees were bent to the chest, the head to the knees, and the position secured with rope. The body was placed in a sitting position or on its side in a grave, or above ground in a cave, or inside a pen of rocks and earth. There was little mourning for old people, but mourning for younger ones and especially for hunters and warriors was long, loud, and accompanied by self-mutilation. Because Comanches lived constantly amid violence and danger, they were not afraid of death.

XI

Religion and Organization

THE COMANCHES BELIEVED there was only one Great Spirit, whom they addressed as such or as "Our Sure-Enough Father." They looked upon the sun, moon, and earth as semideities. In the beginning, they believed, the Great Spirit gathered dust from the four corners of the earth before he made the first man. That way, the earth could not refuse man a burying place. Next the Great Spirit made human bones from stones, blood from dew, eyes from clear water, thoughts from waterfalls, breath from the wind, and strength from storms.

The first man was so gigantic in size that his head touched the sky and he could look from one end of the earth to the other. Hard work and hunger whittled him down to his present size. The Great Spirit taught this creature how to make bows and arrows and stone knives and points, and how to start fire by rubbing two sticks together. Then he put buffalo and other food sources on earth for man's use.

A Comanche legend relates that as man multiplied, the Earth asked the Great Spirit how the multitudes were to be fed. The Great Spirit replied, "We will divide the maintenance of man. You will feed man during the daytime with all that you produce. When the night will come, I will send my sleep upon man. He will rest, and he will be fed by me with the peace of slumber, and he will awake refreshed in the morning."

The Comanches believed the Great Spirit lived beyond the Sun, which nurtured life. Through prayers, Earth, who was their "Mother," was implored to make the water flow so that all living things might drink, to make the ground firm so that creatures might walk on it, and to cause the grass to grow so that buffalo and horses would be fed. The Moon was a lesser deity, and the guardian of raiders. If they planned a horse-stealing expedition, they laid a rope in a circle on the ground, sat inside it, and prayed to the Moon to let the rope encircle many horses.

The Sun, Moon, and Earth were too powerful to serve as an individual's guardian spirits, so they were tribal deities only. An individual's spirits dwelt in rivers, hills, springs, in rocks or trees, in strong birds or animals. Thunder and lightning were not spirits, but caused by the gigantic Thunderbird. This dark-blue bird had red zigzag markings extending from its breast to its tail and wing tips. Its shadow was the thundercloud. It produced lightning by blinking its eyes, and made thunder by flapping its wings. A heavy downpour came from the lake carried on its back. Comanches of all ages feared thunder and lightning, and remained very quiet during a storm so that nothing they said or did would offend the Thunderbird.

Guardian spirits were not the only sources of power. At times Comanches relied on the "little men." They were spirits not more than a foot high who were armed with bows and arrows and shields, and killed with every shot. However, their power was so terribly strong that few men wanted to possess it. It might make a man do something he really didn't want to do, such as killing a friend or relative.

Comanche religious practice was an individual matter. There was no formalized creed or catechism, no priestly class, and no group rituals such as the Kiowa's Sun Dance. Each teen-age boy sought a vision in order that he might recognize the source of his spirit power; that is, a certain hill, or lake, or animal. Unless he had a special spirit of his own, he could not possibly become a successful hunter or warrior.

Usually a youth was about fifteen when he first sought a vision. He bathed as an act of purification, put on only his breechclout and moccasins, and gathered four articles: a buffalo robe, a bone pipe, tobacco or its substitute, and materials for lighting the pipe. He walked off to an isolated spot, preferably a hilltop, halting four times to smoke and pray. That night he slept under the robe with his face toward the east. At dawn he awakened and prayed for power. For four days and nights he fasted and prayed, showing respect for the supernatural powers but never groveling before them. When the vision came, the youth then knew who his guardian spirit was, what magic articles he must put in his medicine bag, and what taboos he must observe from then on. For instance, he might be told that a certain object had the power to make him strong, or that he must never use crow feathers in his arrows.

The powers an individual gained through his vision varied in strength, depending on how much the recipient used them. For the rest of his life a boy or man sought a vision whenever he needed special help before going on a hunt or on the warpath, or plotting revenge on an enemy, or curing an illness. If a man seemed to develop strong curing powers, he became a medicine man. If an appeal was made properly, he could pass his power along to another individual. And, if a power became too strong and its possession a burden, the owner could return to the place where he had received his vision, thank the spirits for letting him use it, and return it to them!

Warriors wore amulets or charms to protect them, and always carried a medicine bag filled with magical articles. It might contain a bit of grass that was considered protective, herbs for their healing power, a claw or bear's snout to inspire courage, small pebbles to insure a long life, and a bit of dried buffalo stomach to help him be fierce in battle. Women also wore charms and owned small medicine bags, and they prayed to individual spirits for strength to carry on all their chores and for strong sons.

Pain and sicknesses were thought to be inflicted by evil spirits. Ailments were treated with prayers and herbal teas, or by applying special salves, or by drumming, or by blowing smoke over the sick person. Medicine men used all sorts of mumbo-jumbo and sleight-of-hand tricks to "draw out" sticks or stones from a body, thus effecting a cure. The pain of rheumatism was relieved by having the patient lie under covers in a rocky trench that had been heated, then strewn with sage and sprinkled with water which produced soothing steam. Broken bones were encased in splints, and tourniquets staunched bleeding. Crude surgical techniques were employed to remove arrowheads. For toothache, a tree fungus was heated and held to the aching jaw. Cavities were packed with powdered mushroom, inflammations covered with poultices, and rashes smeared with a salve made from natural petroleum, which oozed from the ground in certain areas. Many Comanches succumbed to diseases now recognized as pneumonia and tuberculosis, but the greatest killers were the smallpox and cholera introduced by white men. Epidemics killed hundreds and in some instances wiped out entire bands.

Comanches strongly believed in life after death in a realm beyond the setting sun. It was very much like their earth home, except there were no extremes of temperature, no rain, wind, or darkness. All the great chiefs assembled there, and the warriors were forever young and vigorous. Of course buffalo and antelope were in abundance, and horses marvelously fleet. However, after a pleasant sojourn in this place, the Comanche's spirit must be reborn on earth in order to maintain the tribe's population.

The Comanches never developed a strong tribal organization, because they placed such great emphasis on individual freedom and initiative. Each family group had its head man, and each sub-group or band its civil or "peace" chief. These men gained their position by their goodness of character, wisdom, and ability to speak well. (A Comanche rarely made a speech at a tribal council or peace parley without rehearsing it many times.) The chieftanship was not hereditary, nor was it sought competitively. A civil chief's authority depended on persuasion and counseling. Actually, he was a revered patriarch. He was allowed a personal attendant, a crier who announced his recommendations to the people. He also had a staff of young men who served as his bodyguards.

Important decisions affecting the bands were decided in a council made up of warriors and prominent men, the older having rank over the younger. Teen-age boys were permitted to attend council, but only as observers and students. If they spoke out, their fathers would be mortified, and have to make amends for the insult. On rare occasions, wise and able women could attend a council and even express an opinion. The meetings were carried on with great formality. Questions and answers had to be phrased in polite language. Wrangling was never tolerated, nor was a speaker interrupted. Decisions cen-

The ability to speak well in council, highly valued among Comanches, was an important qualification of the men chosen to be their chiefs.

tered on such matters as to when and where to move camp or join in a communal hunt, or how to allocate supplies or divide spoils from a raid, and how best to trade with outsiders. Decisions had to be unanimous, and the people so respected their head men that disobeying them was unthinkable.

Each band had its war chief, whose duties will be described in the following chapter. The people believed strongly in the separation of civil and military power, and considered the best form of government was that which governed the least. While there were no courts or judges, individuals did possess certain rights, and could call hearings in which they made appeals for redress against wrongs suffered. Wife-stealing was one of the worst crimes, and brought severe penalties. Murder was practically unheard of, but if committed, it was considered strictly a family matter. The victim's relatives quickly killed either the murderer or a member of his family, and the matter was considered settled then and there. The situation never developed into a feud. Since Comanches shared their belongings, which included wives, horses, and captives, there was little thievery.

Mention must be made of Comanche treatment of captives. Some adult captives were tortured and slain, but teen-agers or younger children fared well. They were considered chattel property, and belonged to their captor until adopted as brothers if they were boys, or married to him if they were girls. The new relationship was solemnized by mixing blood taken from the vein on the back of the hand of both parties. Until a captive gained this new status, he was cared for and protected by the owner. A captive, being property, could be sold or traded or even killed. During the eighteenth century, most were Mexicans. Being industrious, they were a welcome addition as workers. A few became warriors, and thereby gained membership in the tribe as free men, with all the rights and privileges of adult males. The "naturalization" ceremony was every bit as solemn and formal as a modern-day one in which immigrants become American citizens.

To describe Comanche government and law in its briefest terms, you could say there were as few laws as possible, and enforcement of them remained the responsibility of the individual.

XII

Warriors and Warfare

FROM THE TIME a Comanche boy was a toddler, his life was focused on becoming a warrior. He had no other choice, because his rank as a man in Comanche society depended on the glory and plunder he gained in fighting and raiding.

Instruction began when he was five or six years old, and was geared first toward teaching him to become a skilled horseman and hunter. Since his father was away for weeks at a time on raids, the child's education was the responsibility of a grandfather. The relationship between the two became very close as the grandson learned to ride, shoot a small bow and arrow, make weapons, and hunt small animals. The father assisted when he was home, and so did older brothers, uncles, and cousins, but only if they were seasoned warriors. At this stage they impressed on the child that hunting was very serious work, on which depended the good life of the family and the tribe. Thus the boy learned to become patient, quiet, and extremely cautious, to approach a quarry with stealth and read "signs" (tracks or droppings) under varying weather conditions. An equally important phase of his training dealt with riding and how to rope, break, train, and steal horses.

When a boy entered his teens, he became an apprentice

warrior. He now practiced marksmanship with full-sized weapons, and as part of actual fighting tactics, he learned how to use a horse as a shield. While circling enemies or a number of covered wagons drawn into a circle, the warrior slipped a rawhide loop over his head and under his right arm. The loop was attached to the saddle or plaited into his horse's mane. Then he put his left big toe or foot into another loop and, thus supported, dropped to the far side of his mount and had both hands free for shooting. The horse's body protected him from arrows and bullets. If his mount was wounded or stumbled, the warrior whipped off the loops and leaped free with breathtaking speed and dexterity. Seconds later a comrade would pick him up on the run, and the two then carried on the attack riding double.

The most difficult and dangerous task was learning how to ride swiftly across a battle site and, singly or with the help of a comrade, pick up a wounded or dead warrior and carry him off. This maneuver took years of practice. At first the youth learned to retrieve small light-weight objects at a trotting pace. Gradually the objects became bulkier and heavier and the horse's speed was quickened until the rider could lift a prostrate body from the ground and lay it over his horse. Warriors looked upon this feat as obligatory, because leaving a stricken comrade to be mutilated and scalped by the enemy dishonored both the warriors and their families. Also, the spirit of a scalped person could not enter the spirit world beyond the setting sun, so it was essential that his body be recovered and given a proper burial.

The bow and arrow were the prime weapons. An accomplished marksman attained exceptional accuracy over a distance of fifty yards, and good aim at three hundred yards. An expert could hit a three-inch-wide target four out of five shots

As an apprentice warrior, a Comanche boy practiced using his horse as a shield.

from a distance of 150 paces. A warrior's next important possession was his shield. It was circular, made of tough buffalo hide and decorated with paint, feathers, and any other flickering articles that would confuse the opponent's aim. The shield was carried to ward off arrows and spear thrusts, and also for the magic protective powers it might possess. Among some bands the shields were never carried into the tepees, or hung beside them, or uncovered except in battle. Their power was thought to be so great that they had to be hung on a shrub or tree at a distance, and approached with reverential caution.

The lance was also a favored weapon. The wooden shaft was about six to seven feet long, the point tipped with iron. It might or might not be stored in a beaded sheath. Contrary to the way Indians in Hollywood films brandish their lances, it was never hurled, but thrust underhand. This necessitated close proximity to the enemy, so only the bravest fighters used lances. A warrior involved in hand-to-hand fighting could not retreat. Either he won over his opponent, or died on the spot. On returning from war, a lucky lancer set his weapon upright by the tepee door. No one but he could remove the scalps dangling from it. A lance was thought to carry such responsibility that an aging warrior, still able to fight with bow and arrow, might give his away to a younger man without suffering loss of rank.

An equally deadly weapon was the war club, or tomahawk. The head was usually made of flint stone, about six inches long and three inches wide, with the ends thinned to a rough edge. The stone was grooved so that it could be bound onto a wooden handle some fourteen inches long. As with the lance, only the bravest warriors fought with war clubs.

A warrior's rank and reputation depended on how many times he counted coup, and the quality of the deed. A coup

Comanches never left the bodies of their dead or wounded warriors on the battlefield. Here they bring back a wounded chief.

was the act of touching or hitting an enemy with the hand or weapon. Killing an enemy with a lance or club rated higher than shooting him from a distance. Scalping counted only when the trophy was taken under dangerous conditions. Sometimes two warriors could count coup on the same victim, but none could earn credits by striking an insensible or dead enemy. If a warrior claimed a coup and others proved he was lying, he found himself disgraced. Whenever he killed an enemy, the warrior shouted "*a he!*"—meaning "I claim it." The most honored coup was that earned by removing a wounded or dead comrade from the scene of a fight. Of course warriors who sneaked across enemy lines to kill or steal horses earned coups. Actually, any daring deed that took great personal courage earned a credit. The more coups a warrior earned, the greater his prestige and the better his chance of becoming a war chief.

Scalping was not as highly rated as white men thought it was. After all, anybody could scalp a dead man. Scalping counted only when the trophy was taken at the risk of the warrior's life. Preferably the trophy was the entire scalp. But if a warrior was in a hurry or harassed during the fight, he need cut only a small section. Small or large, the trophy was displayed on a lance during the Scalp Dance. Later a small one might be sewed to the warrior's shirt, shield, or tomahawk.

White men were also misinformed on how a Comanche raid got under way. A warrior didn't just shout the idea on the spur of the moment, leap on his horse, and race off to kill. Though the victims might describe an attack as a hit-and-run affair, most were planned in detail. First the warrior had a vision or dream that prompted his desire to lead a raid, and informed him when and how to attack. After he wakened, he did not make an announcement until the plan was clear in his mind. Then he made medicine by praying and singing, called his friends to his tepee, and discussed the project. When he lighted his pipe and passed it around, those who did not wish to join him handed the pipe on without smoking it. The warrior could also make his intentions known by putting on his war paint and sitting in his tepee, drumming and singing a war song. Those who would accompany him joined in the music. About sunset all mounted their horses and paraded through the village, enlisting more volunteers. A war party could range from four to forty warriors, the size depending on the leader's prestige and the proposed target. If the planned raid was popular with the people, they turned out to sing and encourage the warriors.

After dark a War Dance was held. One historian has described this as comparable to a school pep rally preceding a ball game. After the dance the warriors withdrew to a rendezvouz site, where their ponies and weapons awaited them. From that moment the raid officially was under way. Each warrior provided his own weapons, robe, horses, and dried meat. Sometimes, if the party was to travel a long distance, one or two women went along to attend to camp chores.

Each day on the trail the men gathered in a circle around the leader, who drew a map in the dirt to show landmarks and the next campsite. He was the dictator, and was obeyed implicitly. The warriors knew he would never ask them to do something he would not tackle himself. Although they might make suggestions, the leader planned the time and location of the rest stops, the placing of scouts and guards, the approach and attack and withdrawal. It was his responsibility to head the attack, signal the withdrawal, or if necessary make a truce with the enemy.

One or two scouts always moved a day's ride ahead of the main party. The latter, rarely traveling at night, rode steadily and quietly across the country. After the night meal the leader brought out his pipe, offered appropriate prayers, and passed it to his warriors. Then all rolled up in their robes and slept.

When the party came close to its target, scouts moved ahead to view the area. On their return the leader and his men set forth. If this was a horse-stealing raid, they moved in pairs. Their first task was to silence the guards. Then the older warriors slipped into the herd and quietly cut out the best horses, which usually were picketed. The younger men gathered the loose horses. If an alarm sounded and a fight developed, the younger men ran the horses off while the more experienced warriors whooped up the attack and kept it going until the horses were out of reach. Then they peeled off and speedily joined their companions at a pre-arranged site. The leader passed the pipe, thanked each man, and divided the booty. He kept only a small portion for himself, because he profited more from the glory of conducting a successful raid. A selfish leader might find few men willing to join him on another raid.

An attack on an isolated ranch, a camp of enemy Indians or of white buffalo hunters, a wagon train, or a small company of soldiers was handled a little differently. The leader rode at the front of a wedge-shaped body of warriors, who counted on the suddenness of their attack, speed, and terrifying war-whoops to work to their victims' disadvantage. If the latter stood their ground and a counterattack developed, the warriors circled their prey, coming in closer with each full revolution. On signal from the leader, they slipped to the far side of their mounts and began shooting. If a horse was shot down, the rider jumped free, grabbed his shield and continued shooting from behind his fallen mount. A favorite tactic was to make the victims fire too soon, and then charge in for the kill while they were frantically reloading.

Whenever possible, the Comanches avoided a pitched battle. They rarely attacked an outfit equal to or larger than theirs. If charged, their line opened and dropped back, and then swiftly closed in on the flanks and rear of the enemy. An attack lasted until their ponies tired and the enemy fire proved too costly. Then they retrieved their wounded and withdrew a short distance to rest for a second or third charge. If drawn into toe-to-toe combat, the Comanches fought as desperately and ferociously as any other plains Indians. They expected no quarter, gave none, and never surrendered.

Their only prisoners were women and children, and they kept only a few. All others were killed, because a war party had no way to imprison its captives, nor food enough to sustain them during the long journey back to their village. There the prisoners might be tortured to death. Yet there were numerous instances of Comanches treating captives fairly well and later accepting them into their families. Usually they demanded ransom payments before surrendering white captives. But Comanche conduct was never predictable.

If any warriors had been killed on the raid, their bodies were buried secretly along the return trail. When the party came in sight of their village, the men painted their faces black and shaved off their horses' tails, and slipped quietly into their lodges. As the sad word spread, the women started howling, tearing their hair and clothing, and slashing their arms. In contrast, if the raid had been successful and no casualties suffered, the leader sent a message ahead to inform the people of their arrival. Then both warriors and the people donned their finest regalia and face paint, and the returning heroes were greeted with songs and cheers. That evening a Victory Dance, or a Scalp Dance if scalps had been taken, was held. The warriors were also given all the time they needed to brag about their deeds.

The combination of superior intelligence and stamina, a bountiful supply of food and goods, and a life style totally devoted to waging war inevitably produced the most fearsome rapacious raiders ever seen in Texas. For a century and a half the Comanches were the undisputed lords of the southern plains.

XIII

Lords of the Plains

AFTER THE COMANCHES gained horses and fighting superiority, they warred incessantly. Some bands fought the Ute Indians throughout the Great Basin. The Utes allied with the Jicarilla Apaches, who ranged the upper reaches of the Rio Grande River. After putting them to route, the Comanches moved eastward. They assaulted the Lipan Apaches, the most eastern Apache people encountered by Coronado in his trek across New Mexico and the Texas Panhandle. During the sixteenth and seventeenth centuries, the Lipan Apaches had dominated this portion of present-day Texas and should be included among the Indians of Texas, but unfortunately almost nothing is known of their campsites or their life within the state's boundaries.

At the time the above was taking place, other Comanches began migrating southeastward onto the Great Plains. Here they fought with roving Cheyenne bands and Arapahoes and especially with the Pawnees in what is now Nebraska. As they moved down the Arkansas, Cimarron, and Canadian rivers, they became involved in a long and bloody war with the Kiowas. These tall handsome Indians had been forced out of the Yellowstone River country by the Dakota Sioux. They had been joined by a small eastern Apache group, who may have separated from the Lipan Apaches. For an undetermined period the Kiowas and their allies, now called the Kiowa Apaches, fought the Comanches. Finally the chiefs realized the senselessness of the slaughter, and in 1790 they agreed to stop fighting each other. The resulting alliance remained strong throughout the years when both tribes were displaced by the white Anglo-American pioneer settlers, and were nearly exterminated in their war with the Federal troops.

Some scholars consider the Kiowas and Kiowa Apaches as Indians of Texas. Others do not because for the most part these people are identified primarily with southern Kansas, the panhandle of Oklahoma and the Wichita Mountains. Some hunted along the Canadian River in the Texas Panhandle, and joined the Comanches in raids against the settlers. But because the Kiowas were active in such a small area of Texas and their principal villages were outside the present boundaries, they will not be described in this book. Since they were plains nomads and buffalo hunters, their way of life was similar in many ways to that of the Comanches. When the Army finally defeated them, the impoverished survivors were forced to settle on a Federal reservation in southwestern Oklahoma, and their further involvement in Texas history came to an end.

When the Comanches dispossessed the Apaches from the southernmost plains, the Apaches formed an alliance with the Spaniards. This act so enraged the Comanches that they attacked the Spanish mission and presidio on the San Saba River, near present-day Menard, Texas. Their sudden furious assault quickly overwhelmed the inept soldiers and mission Indians. In retaliation the Spaniards mounted an expedition and attacked a large Comanche village camped near the site of Ringgold. Their clumsy armor and blundering guns were no match for the yowling copper-skinned bowmen, and they were nearly annihilated. Enormously inflated by this victory and avid for more Spanish blood and horses, the Comanches pounced on one Spanish settlement after another. In San Antonio they paraded through the dusty streets in all their savage finery, shouting insults and pillaging at will. But they still were not satisfied, and extended their raiding into northern Mexico.

At first the horses gained on these forays were traded for manufactured goods in New Mexico. Later a good many were sold to the members of the Anglo-American colony established in 1823 by Stephen Austin at San Felipe, northwest of Houston. Since the Americans were few in number then, and friendly, the Comanches tolerated their presence. This, of course, gave the colonists time to increase in number and strength. By 1830 there were more Anglo-Americans in the region than Comanches. Unlike the all-male Spanish expeditions, which came to conquer and exploit the natives and virtually enslaved them, these settlers brought their families and worked the land themselves. They spread out across the country from Caddo-land to Comanchería, taking over the Indians' favorite campsites, raising cabins, driving off the buffalo, and plowing up the native grass. The Comanches took offense, and thus began the long, bitter struggle between the two for the possession of central and western Texas. Since both peoples were aggressive and intolerant of one another, bloodshed was inevitable.

When the Americans brought in large strong horses, far superior to the runty mustangs that had developed from the original Spanish stock, the Comanches not only stole them; they lifted a few scalps as a bonus. One raid led to another, and another, and another. The best-known of these was the attack in May 1836 by northern Comanches and their Kiowa allies on Parker's Fort, a stockade seventy miles east of Waco. Several whites were killed and five captives taken, including Parker's nine-year-old daughter, Cynthia Ann. The Comanches never released her, although ransom money was offered repeatedly. At first the neighbors claimed the attack was uncalled-for. Later, however, Parker was accused of having helped the Indians earlier in their horse-stealing expeditions against the settlers and then cheating them of their share of the money gained from the sale. Presumably the Indians got even by attacking Parker's stockade. (The site is now a state park.)

On April 21, 1836, General Sam Houston and the Texas army defeated the Mexican army at San Jacinto, near Houston. This much-acclaimed victory gained Texas freedom from Mexico. It also made a deep impression on the Comanches, because it made all too clear to them the power the whites could summon against armed aggressors. Three months after being chosen president of the free and independent Republic of Texas, Houston sent a delegation to parley with the Comanches. The leader carried a letter from Houston, which read in part:

COMANCHE CHIEFS—BROTHERS.

You as well as the Americans have always been free and never conquered. Your enemies and ours are the same. I send you my friends to talk to you—to give you presents and to make peace with you and your people.

You have many things to trade and to swap with us. You need many things that we can let you have cheaper than you have ever been able to get them from the Mexicans. You can let us have horses, mules and buffalo robes in change for our paints, tobacco, blankets, and other things which will make you happy. I wish to have a smooth path, that shall lead from your camp to my house, that we can meet each other, and that it shall never become bloody.

Houston concluded by inviting the chiefs to a treaty council.

The more mature Comanche warriors had developed a grudging respect for the Americans, and thus could see the advantage of an alliance. But the younger warriors would have nothing to do with treaty talk. Actually, they were acting from self-interest, because only by accumulating war honors could they enhance their personal wealth and rank.

After months of haranguing in village councils, a number of chiefs and warriors traveled to San Antonio for peace talks. Because they felt equal to the white men, the chiefs didn't mince words. If Sam Houston wanted peace, they said, then these were their terms: they insisted on recognition of their rights to certain lands. The white commissioners refused to concede that the Indians had any prior rights in Texas. Next the Comanches proposed that a boundary line be drawn beyond which Americans could neither hunt nor take up residence. The whites would not accept a boundary line, but did promise to appoint a white agent who would "protect" the Indians from white trespassers in the future and, at the same time, supervise trade between the two nations. The Comanches did not feel they needed protection, but were interested in expanding their trade with the whites. After days of haggling the two parties finally signed a treaty, on May 29, 1838.

When the Texas Senate failed to ratify it, however, the Comanches concluded that the Texans were not keeping faith with them. And, as still more white families poured into their domain, they resumed raiding. Both sides were bent on exterminating or driving out the other.

In 1838, Mirabeau B. Lamar succeeded Houston as president of the Republic. He recommended an all-out war be waged against the Comanches. The Texas Congress promptly supplied one thousand men with arms, and appropriated the impressive sum of one million dollars to garrison a string of frontier forts. More raids and counterattacks resulted.

Within a year some Penatekas (southern Comanches) were so hard pressed that they sent emissaries to San Antonio to arrange a peace parley. The Texas commissioners were agreeable, so in the spring of 1840 sixty-five men, women, and children arrived. On March 19 the top-ranking head men and white officials gathered inside a building, the women and children remaining outside. After the usual tedious and stilted greetings, the powwow got under way.

Arguments soon flared when, the Texans having demanded the Indians surrender their white captives, the Penatekas handed over one prisoner, declaring this was all they had. An army officer angrily accused them of lying and retaining additional captives. He tried to intimidate them by ordering armed troops to enter the council chamber and arrest the chiefs, so that they could be detained as hostages until more whites were released. The unarmed Indians felt betrayed and sprang up to fight for their lives. Before the smoke cleared from the room and adjoining courtyard, thirty-five Penatekas, including three women and two children, were dead, and seven whites had been killed and eight wounded.

When word of the Council House tragedy, as it was called, reached other bands of southern Comanches, they tortured their white prisoners to death and went on a terrible rampage. The Texas militia hit them hard in several engagements, notably at Plum Creek, near present-day Lockhart, and in a surprise night raid on a hunting camp. They killed 130 Indians and captured 34 women and children. Neighboring bands were so stunned that they withdrew westward, in an effort to avoid further contact with the whites. For the first time in their lives, these southern Comanches found their life style reversed. Now they were in jeopardy rather than the aggressors. Now they were the hunted, the displaced. This painful realization gnawed at their arrogance and began to erode their proud spirits.

Any hope of mutual peace and understanding between the two adversaries was blocked by two factors. First, neither really wanted peace. While both gave lip service to the desirability of living peacefully side by side, each was determined to be rid of the other. A rich prize was at stake, namely, the domination of the vast inland plains empire we know today as the state of Texas. Sharing it with a despised enemy was unthinkable.

Second, effective communication was hampered by the language barrier. Dialogues and negotiations were conducted through interpreters, whose bungling translations, sometimes deliberately devious, created a climate of mistrust between the parties. Since the Comanches had no written language, they resented having to place their marks on a document which they could not read. At first they accepted the solemn word of the white commissioners that the terms written into the treaty were really those agreed upon verbally. Unfortunately, this was not always the case. The Indians were misled or downright cheated on occasion, and so in time they came to distrust anything white men said or wrote down.

Nowadays apologists try to prove that all the blame for Indian-white conflicts were caused by the whites. This is not true in regard to the Comanches. Both sides shared the blame. The Comanches were as changeable as the Texas weather. They were first and foremost *Komantcia*—that is, enemies.

They came to many a council only to obtain the gifts promised them, and had no more intention of abiding by treaty agreements than the whites. And since both rivals would not accept peaceful coexistence, the conflict raged until the lords of the southern plains suffered overwhelming defeat.

XIV

Deterioration

ON DECEMBER 29, 1845, Texas was admitted as the twenty-eighth state of the Union, and annexation formalities were completed on February 16, 1846. Soon after, the citizens demanded that the Federal government "do something" about the Indian problem. The government complied by offering the southern Comanches expensive gifts if they would attend a council. Perhaps because the Indians who appeared at the council were dealing with Federal officials, whom they considered *Americans* and not Texans, they agreed to stop the raiding. This was extremely important because the United States was moving toward a war with Mexico and needed to concentrate its forces in that conflict. The government, however, authorized the state of Texas to raise nine companies of civilians for frontier defense, ensuring the state a period of peace. But after the United States won her war with Mexico, the old hostility with the Indians flared anew.

A disastrous epidemic of cholera and smallpox hit many Comanche villages in 1849 and 1850. The diseases were introduced by whites en route to the California gold fields. One route began at San Antonio and Austin, the state capital. The Comanches had been run out of this area, and now freight wagons, stagecoaches, and mail expresses moved regularly between Houston and the two settlements. West of Austin the "California road" crossed the domain of the Penatekas or Wasps on the way to El Paso. Because the gold-seekers traveled in large, well-armed companies, the Indians refrained from attacks, and visited their encampments to trade. There they became infected with the diseases. Within six months many bands were wiped out. Those that survived were too weak to make trouble, and signed a peace treaty with the government.

The northern Comanches also became infected when three thousand Argonauts traveled west up the Red River valley and across the Texas Panhandle toward California. The Antelopes, Wanderers, and Buffalo-eaters suffered severe losses as epidemics ravaged their villages. Although they did not realize it at the time, they also suffered in other ways. Heretofore there had been little traffic across their hunting grounds. White men believed wagon trains or hunting parties could not travel across the Staked Plains without becoming lost on the featureless plain. But after the route had been marked by the ashes of the Argonauts' campfires, and the location of water holes determined, this far-flung wilderness attracted many settlers. In addition, as other settlers moved in from the east and south, they forced the Tejas, Wichitas, Wacos, and Tonkawas to withdraw into Comanche territory. As a result, the lords of the plains found themselves fighting both whites and Indians. Much as they liked fighting, this was too much!

The Comanches lost ground in other ways, too. The buffalo, their prime source of food and robes, became scarce because of the deliberate campaign of overkill perpetrated by the settlers. They knew full well that if they rid the country of the buffalo and other wild game, the Indians eventually would starve. The mounting scarcity forced the Comanches to travel longer distances to locate the dwindling herds. Being on the move so much and trying to keep their camps hidden from the soldiers gave the people less time for preserving food and making clothing and weapons. Since their better campsites and watering holes had been taken over by white ranchers, the Comanches had to camp in areas where water, wood, and grass for their large herds of horses were in scant supply. Thus the quality of Comanche life deteriorated.

And this was not all. Some Comanche raiders had made yearly forays into northern Mexico for horses, captives, and goods, and they now encountered triple trouble: from the Mexican Army, the Texas Rangers, and patrols of the all-Negro United States Ninth Cavalry, stationed in southwestern Texas. They now acquired less loot to swap for manufactured goods traded by the *comancheros*. (These were white traders who accepted stolen goods in exchange for kettles, blankets, tobacco, sugar, and such contraband articles as whiskey, rifles, and ammunition. The *comancheros* had no qualms about furnishing the Indians with weapons that would be used against white settlers.)

As all this trouble engulfed them, the Comanches were losing many valuable fighting men who could not be replaced readily. After all, it took twenty years to produce and train a warrior. In contrast, the government manned eight frontier garrisons between the Canadian River and the Rio Grande. By 1853 the number of Indian raids dropped to almost nothing, thanks to the presence of approximately 3300 Federal troops in Texas. But the Comanches were far from subdued. They bided their time, and gathered strength for a fresh assault. When overconfident military leaders withdrew half the troops two years later, the Comanches rampaged in every direction.

In a desperate effort to settle the problem, the government sought and received enough state land to form two small reservations in the upper Brazos country. The plan was to settle all the Indians left in Texas on the reservations, and provide soldier patrols to keep the Indians inside the boundaries and the whites outside. The weaker tribes, much reduced in number, welcomed the move, but except for five hundred members of a Wasp band, the Comanches refused to accept reservation life. They attacked the reservation Indians so savagely that in 1859 the government moved all the "friendlies" to a distant, safer home in Oklahoma.

The outbreak of the Civil War in 1861 put the Comanches in an advantageous position. Neither the Federal nor the Confederate government could afford to wage war against them. Neither asked them to fight on one side or the other; rather, each bought peace with gifts. Once more the Comanches enjoyed a respite from war and bided their time. When the war ended, the Northern forces were involved outside the state and the Southern forces were broken up. This left the frontier undefended. The Comanches swarmed out like angry hornets. Many Texans died cruelly, and hundreds of thousands of their cattle were stolen and driven into New Mexico for sale to unscrupulous whites. A year passed before troops adequately manned the frontier posts.

The great westward migration of Americans resumed after the close of the Civil War. To prevent more bloodshed, Congress appropriated funds for several parleys at which the government hoped a lasting peace could be negotiated. The largest of these, and the one involving the Comanches, was held on

Medicine Lodge Creek in Kansas in October 1867. Lured by the promise of free beef, coffee, and other gifts, Kiowas, Kiowa Apaches, Arapahoes, Cheyennes, and about one-third of the Comanche bands accepted the invitation. Each tribe presented its people in their richest raiment. They sang, danced, and performed breath-taking feats of horsemanship and marksmanship in order to impress the Federal commissioners, army officers, and soldiers present.

When the head men sat down to talk, each tribe was given time to air its complaints and petition for redress from losses suffered at the hands of the whites. The commissioners presented the case for the settlers, hunters, and freighters. One fact became clear. Both factions wanted an end to conflict. The whites wanted to travel through the Indian country without loss of lives or property. *So did the Indians.*

After much haranguing the government promised to pay the various tribes for the right to build wagon roads and railroads across their territory, and for land to be opened for settlement. These payments would be made annually, partly in cash and partly in supplies. In exchange, the Indians would be let alone *if they gave up their freedom* and settled on a large reservation, which would extend from the Arkansas River in Kansas down through western Oklahoma to the Red River. The army would station troops there to keep white men from hunting buffalo or running their cattle on the reservation, from molesting the Indians, and from peddling whiskey to them.

Most of the chieftans present signed the treaty, thus ending their tribes' status as free and independent people. Had they refused to do so, they would have received no "annuities," as the payments and supplies were called, and soldiers would have rounded them up like cattle and forced them onto the

At Medicine Lodge Creek, Comanches and other tribes met with government officials in 1867 and made a treaty establishing a reservation north of the Red River.

reservation. On the other hand, the reservation included almost three million acres of wide rolling plains surrounding the beautiful Wichita Mountains. It was a region still rich in timber, grass, and wild game, with ample rainfall and not too severe winters. Each tribe was assigned a portion for its own use. The Comanches and Kiowas shared the southwest sector.

The agency from which the goods would be distributed was built in southwestern Oklahoma. It included a store, warehouse, and housing for the agent and his helpers. Three miles away a new frontier post, named Fort Sill, was erected and manned with companies of another all-Negro regiment, the Tenth Cavalry. These troops were to maintain order on the reservation, and patrol the Red River boundary to prevent whites from trespassing and Indians from slipping off across the river into Texas.

The government officials were enormously pleased with the program they had designed for peace on the frontier. Unfortunately, it did not work, because neither side kept its word. At first the Indians acted in good faith. Those who settled on the reservation were confident they would be looked after. But trouble rose immediately when the agent said they must sell off their pony herds and become farmers. He distributed seeds and tools, and showed them how to farm. The braves sneered. Farming was squaw work! They would have none of it. And give up their horses? Never!

Then the payment of annuities was delayed many months. The quality of the goods, when finally distributed, was disgraceful. Dishonest contractors had enriched themselves by furnishing shoddy clothing that tore like paper, wormy flour, and rancid meat. By this time the wild game close by had been thinned out by overhunting. Even though the families were

A Comanche village about 1870, soon after the tribe had settled on the reservation.

starving, the men learned they could not leave the reservation to hunt.

The older chiefs who tried to abide by the restrictions found their authority challenged by the younger warriors. Now for the first time there was great dissension within the bands. The younger men ridiculed the chiefs, called them cowards, and ignored them. A good many slipped off in the darkness, crossed the Red River, and sought buffalo in the old way. But white hunters had killed literally millions of the beasts for their hides, leaving the carcasses to rot on the plains. The small, gun-shy herds were difficult to locate.

The young warriors worked themselves into a frenzy. They had been brought up to be hunters and warriors. Their rank and personal wealth depended on the spoils of hunting and warfare. Now they were denied buffalo trophies and the excitement that accompanied the old-time communal hunts and hunting dances. They were also denied the tremendous satisfaction of providing plenty of meat and robes for their families. Small wonder they vented their rage on outlying settlers, from whom they took cattle and scalps.

Meantime, whiskey peddlers sneaked onto the reservation and traded their rotgut liquor for fine robes and buckskin garments. The younger braves developed such a craving for liquor that they almost stripped their families of their robes and other belongings. At the same time, cattlemen drove their herds onto the reservation and the grass intended for Indian ponies was consumed by cattle. Then white horse thieves moved in, and stole hundreds of Indian ponies. The troops tried in vain to stem the illicit traffic. They were too few in number, and burdened with too many miles to patrol.

In retaliation the Comanches and Kiowas resumed raiding, and more Texans died. The agent, a Quaker who sincerely

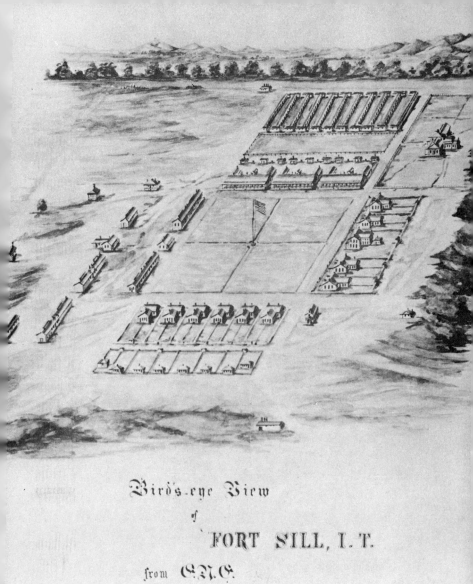

Bird's-eye View

of

FORT SILL, I. T.

from G.N.O.

A new post, Fort Sill, was built near the reservation. Troops of the Tenth Cavalry policed the area and patrolled the boundary.

believed the Indians would change if treated kindly, promised the chiefs more supplies of better quality if they would stop their young men from raiding. When messengers brought word out to them, the young men did slip back to their tepees, and the agent, much pleased, doled out clothing and meat. But after a feast and family reunion, the young raiders took off again.

They were not the only Comanches roaming free. Several bands of northern Comanches, the Antelopes or Kwahadi and the Buffalo-eaters, were determined never to give up their freedom. In the face of mounting odds, they continued their nomadic way of life. More and more, however, they concentrated on stealing cattle and plundering freight wagons. One of their warrior chiefs was Quanah Parker, son of a Kwahadi chief and Cynthia Ann Parker, who had grown up with the band after being kidnaped. Among frontier settlers, the name Quanah Parker soon became a synonym for merciless bloody savagery.

By 1872 the government policy of trying to get the Indians to live peacefully on reservations had proved disastrous. True, had each party lived up to its promises, peace might have come about. Neither had, however, and now the army would mount a campaign aimed at the abject surrender or total extermination of the lords of the southern plains.

XV

Surrender

UNTIL SEPTEMBER of 1872 the renegade Comanche bands plundered widely across the Staked Plains, but their reign of terror was coming to a close. On September 29, Colonel Ranald S. Mackenzie led five companies of the Fourth Cavalry from their camp near Fort Griffin, close by the Clear Fork of the Brazos. With the help of Tonkawa scouts, he located and surprised a large village of 262 lodges strung along McClellan Creek near the mouth of Blanco Canyon. After a hot fight, the surviving warriors fled, leaving 23 Indians dead. The army captured 130 women and children and took possession of over three thousand ponies. The lodges were burned, the household goods destroyed, and the prisoners removed to the reservation. But on the road, the Comanches taught Mackenzie a hard lesson. The warriors attacked and recovered almost all the horses. But the defeat checked further raids until spring.

Then the Comanches renewed their attacks, only to suffer additional setbacks. This frightened them so that they prayed to the Great Spirit for help. Not long after, a young untried warrior called Ishatai (Coyote Droppings) had a dream. He claimed to have ascended above the clouds and communed with the Great Spirit. When he told the people in his village, they were awe-struck. Always superstitious, and now groping frantically for a messiah who would bring back their days of glory, they rejected their chief and turned to Ishatai for leadership. As messengers carried word of his vision to neighboring bands, many more became convinced that obeying Ishatai was the only way to Comanche salvation.

The following spring Ishatai had another vision. He said that if all Comanches came together for a Sun Dance, they would learn how to regain their power. Again the word went out to all the bands. In May 1874, for the first time in their tribe's history, the Comanches gathered together. Many Kiowas and Kiowa Apaches were invited to join in the religious festival. It was held in a far corner of the reservation where no prying soldiers could spy on the ceremony. Prayerfully the people erected a large lodge for the dance. After the warriors had undergone a ritual of purification and donned their finest suits and headdresses, they led the parade inside the lodge and took their places around a center pole. Then for four days and nights, without food or water and with few rest periods, the warriors shuffled and stomped about while the older men thumped the drums and the women sang.

At the conclusion Ishatai announced that if the warriors took to the warpath in one massive raid, they could kill all the whites in Comanchería. After that was accomplished, he promised, the buffalo would return by the thousands and good times would enrich every family. On hearing this the people screeched and worked themselves into a frenzy. Five hundred warriors, including some Kiowas, Kiowa Apaches, and Cheyennes, donned their fighting regalia and war paint, and galloped off to start their war of extermination.

Their first target was a camp of buffalo hunters located on a creek flowing into the Canadian River, in Hutchinson County, Texas. At daybreak on June 24 they assaulted the small adobe-walled buildings, which housed twenty-six men. The latter barricaded the doors and met the wild charge with deadly gunfire. Again and again, that day and for the next two days, the Comanches stormed the walls, but in vain. Then the realization that a handful of white hunters had repulsed the great fighting strength of the Comanche nation was a terrible blow to the warriors' hopes and pride. Badly disillusioned, furious at Ishatai for misleading them, spiritually shaken by the defeat, they gave up the fight and rode away.

An undetermined number slipped back onto the reservation and fought no more. But Quanah Parker rallied the still-rebellious young men and their families, and continued the war. In the following weeks he led them on a strike-and-run campaign against the soldiers who took to the field after the siege on the hunters' post. Now the military commanders had set out on a war of extermination, and companies of well-armed, well-supplied cavalrymen and infantrymen closed in on the renegades from all sides. As the cordon tightened and camp after camp was attacked, the Comanches suffered greatly in the loss of ponies, tepees, and personal belongings. They were like deer trying to outrun the hunters. Some of the women and children died of exhaustion and exposure. The survivors mourned because there was no time to bury the dead properly.

Finally the people sought refuge in a favorite wintering place, Palo Duro Canyon. The fairly steep walls were studded with cedar trees, excellent for badly needed tepee poles and firewood. The floor of the canyon was carpeted in wild grass and watered by a clear stream. Since the canyon could not be seen from the plains surrounding it, it was a perfect hiding place, with deer and game birds and fish enough to feed the hungry people.

The Comanches drove their remaining ponies up to the head of the canyon and raised their tepees or brush shelters along the stream. Below them were a small number of Kiowa families, and about a mile away a few Cheyennes. As days passed peacefully and the scouts on the canyon rim reported no soldiers were approaching, the people relaxed.

Meantime, however, military scouts located the hideaway. Colonel Mackenzie ordered a quiet forced march under cover of darkness. At first light his troops eased down a trail leading to the Comanche camp. A heavy morning mist enveloped the bottom, muffling their footsteps. On signal, they fired on the tepees. As shots exploded about them, the warriors grabbed their weapons and fought desperately, so that their families could flee out of the canyon trap along a secret get-away trail. Because the warriors were outnumbered, they withdrew foot by foot, using boulders and trees for cover as they sniped at the soldiers. The ponies were frightened by the gunfire and milled about, adding to the dust and confusion. Visibility was so poor that advance patrols of soldiers were fired on by their own comrades.

When air currents cleared the canyon about midday, the Indians were gone. The soldiers destroyed their lodges and rounded up the remaining ponies. The next morning the colonel ordered every pony killed, so that the Indians could not steal them out from under his nose again. After the firing ceased, over fourteen hundred lay dead. And shortly after, many of the frightened, starving fugitives were overtaken and forced to walk the many miles to the reservation.

thousand people poured in. Three towns came into being—Lawton, Hobart, and Anadarko, Oklahoma. The last took over the site once occupied by the Indian agency.

Territorial status and then statehood promised a bright future for Oklahoma, but the Comanches, long used to roaming over millions of acres of grassy plains, now were pinned down to a few thousand acres. Overwhelmed with the pressures of civilization which crowded them on all sides, they had only two choices left. Either they submerged their Comanche identity and took up the white man's way of life, or they perished. Some chose one road. The others perhaps found release as their spirits slipped free and sped toward the happier land beyond the sun.

—